P9-AQL-975

Appomattox Regional Library Systems
Hopewell, Virginia 23860
08/02

Those *Extraordinary* *Women* OF WORLD WAR I

Those EXTRAORDINARY WOMEN OF WORLD WAR I

Karen Zeinert

The Millbrook Press
Brookfield, Connecticut

To Jeanne Lee

Published by The Millbrook Press, Inc.
2 Old New Milford Road
Brookfield, Connecticut 06804
www.millbrookpress.com

Cover photograph courtesy of National Archives
Map by Joe LeMonnier

Photographs courtesy of AP/Wide World Photos: pp. 8, 11; © Corbis/Bettmann: pp. 16, 60, 66, 81; © Baldwin H. Ward & Kathryn C. Ward/Corbis: p. 24; Montana Historical Society: p. 27; National Archives: pp. 33 (top), 39, 53, 74 (center); Sophia Smith Collection: p. 33 (bottom); Naval Historical Foundation: p. 41 (#94945); Culver Pictures, Inc.: pp. 44, 70, 74 (bottom); Underwood & Underwood/Corbis: p. 51; Library of Congress: p. 54; YMCA of the USA Archives, University of Minnesota, St. Paul, MN: pp. 68, 72; The Salvation Army: p. 74 (top)

Library of Congress Cataloging-in-Publication Data
Zeinert, Karen.
Those extraordinary women of World War I / Karen Zeinert.
p. cm.
Includes bibliographical references and index.
ISBN 0-7613-1913-1 (lib. bdg.)
World War, 1914–1918—Women—Biography—Juvenile literature.
[1. World War, 1914–1918—Women—Biography. 2. Women—Biography.] I. Title.
D639.W7 Z45 2001
940.3'082—dc21   00-068371

Copyright © 2001 by Karen Zeinert
Printed in Hong Kong
All rights reserved
1 3 5 4 2

CONTENTS

Europe at the time of
World War I: 1914–1918

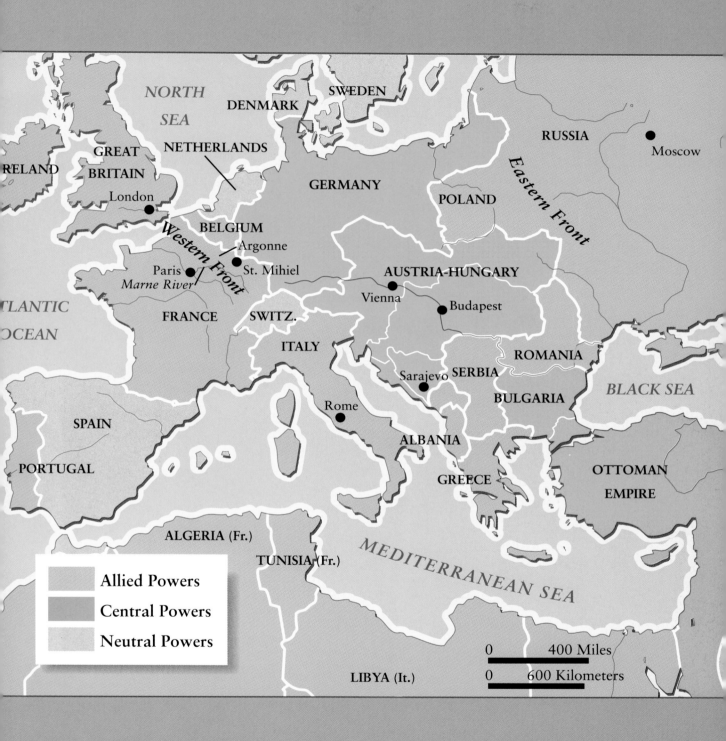

President Woodrow Wilson addresses the special session of Congress assembled on April 2, 1917, urging Congress to declare war on Germany.

CHAPTER ONE

The GREAT WAR

The challenge is to all mankind. . . . The World must be made safe for democracy.

President Woodrow Wilson

On the evening of April 2, 1917, American senators, representatives, and a few specially invited guests gathered in the nation's capital for an extraordinary session of Congress. Outfitted in their best suits and dresses for what they knew was to be an historic event, legislators and guests alike filed to their seats in carefully measured paces. Then the men and women, their expressions reflecting the seriousness of the occasion, turned their eyes toward the speaker's stand and waited in silence for President Woodrow Wilson to arrive.

This momentous session was brought about by a number of shocking events, the first of which took place thousands of miles from America's shores on June 28, 1914. On that fateful day, Austrian Archduke Francis Ferdinand, heir to the throne of the Austrian-Hungarian Empire, and his wife, Sophie, visited Sarajevo, the capital of Bosnia, which was one of the empire's provinces in Central Europe. To welcome the royal couple, officials in the capital had made arrangements for a well-publicized motorcade through the heart of the city. The idea of a procession down Sarajevo's beautifully decorated streets especially pleased Francis Ferdinand and Sophie, so shortly after arriving, they climbed into their designated car, waved to the many people who had lined the streets to get a glimpse of them, and set out for a pleasant ride.

Unfortunately, seven assassins, members of a secret Serbian organization called the Black Hand, waited along the motorcade's route, each hoping for an opportunity to kill the archduke. The first attempt was made by Nedjelko Cabrinovic, who tossed a bomb at the royal couple's automobile when it neared his vantage point. This explosive missed Francis Ferdinand and instead wounded several men in the next car. The archduke's driver, fearing for his passengers' lives, revved the car's engine and raced from the scene. In the process, he roared past three stunned would-be assassins who now had no time to take action.

After reaching safety at city hall, Francis Ferdinand and Sophie, underestimating the danger they faced, decided to visit the wounded men in the hospital. The assassins were still waiting for an opportunity to strike, and when nineteen-year-old Gavrilo Princip saw the archduke's auto approaching him on one of the city's main streets, he seized the moment. Princip ran to the car, pulled out his revolver, and fired away, fatally wounding the archduke and his wife.

Understandably, Austrians were appalled by the assassinations. Not only had Princip taken the life of two defenseless people, one of whom was a woman, but he had also spilled royal blood, which was an unthinkable crime. Someone will pay for this! Austrians shouted as they shook their fists in the air. And they will pay dearly!

Although there was no proof that Serbia had anything to do with the assassination plot, Austria was quick to cast suspicion upon its neighbor. This was due in part to Princip's ties to the Black Hand and in part to an intense hatred that had developed between these two countries over the years. Leaders from both nations had repeatedly argued about many things, including how ethnic Serbs in the empire should be governed, especially those living in Bosnia and Herzegovina. Both provinces, taken by force from the crumbling Ottoman Empire more than thirty years earlier, had been annexed by Austria in 1908 despite vigorous protests from Serbians living in the provinces and expressions of outrage from Serbian officials, who had hoped to add Bosnia and Herzegovina to their nation.

To pacify Serbians in the provinces, Francis Ferdinand had begun to work on a plan to give the empire's newest members more privileges when he became

Sophie Chotek (1868–1914)

Sophie Chotek was born into a royal Czech family that had fallen upon hard times long before she met Archduke Francis Ferdinand. In order to support herself, she became a lady-in-waiting to Archduchess Isabella in Pressburg, Austria.

The archduchess had several daughters, one of whom Francis Ferdinand had begun to court. But after Sophie joined Isabella's royal household, it soon became apparent that the archduke was more interested in Sophie than he was in Isabella's daughter. In a fit of temper, Isabella fired Sophie and then informed the archduke's uncle, the emperor of Austria, Francis Joseph I, about his nephew's infatuation.

The emperor wasted little time in confronting Francis Ferdinand. When the archduke admitted that he had fallen in love with Sophie and that had had every reason to believe that she loved him, the emperor was beside himself. Because Francis Ferdinand was in line to inherit the throne, he had to have the emperor's permission to marry. For more than a year, Francis Joseph I refused even to consider the idea, insisting that the archduke had to take a wife from a royal family of good standing, which did not include the Choteks.

But when the archduke would not change his mind, a compromise was reached. Francis Ferdinand could marry Sophie, but none of their children could ever inherit the throne. In addition, Sophie would never be granted the privileges enjoyed by other members of the royalty. For example, at royal functions when participants entered the reception room in the palace in order of rank, Sophie could not enter until every duchess, countess, and princess, forty-four in all, had presented themselves, and then only after one of the two doors forming the grand entryway had been closed to indicate her lesser rank.

Sophie's lowly position followed her to her grave. She was denied any elaborate decorations at her funeral, and while her coffin was on display, it was placed several feet lower than her husband's, a decision that upset many Austrians who held a much higher opinion of Sophie than the archduke's relatives did. Knowing that Sophie could not be buried in the royal family's plot, Francis Ferdinand had long before stated that upon their eventual deaths he and his wife should be placed in crypts beneath the chapel of his castle, Artstetten. This wish was carried out much sooner than the archduke could have anticipated and without royal objection.

Archduke Ferdinand and Sophie walk to their waiting car on June 28, 1914, the day they would be assassinated.

emperor. Serbian leaders had found out about the archduke's project, and fearing that it would make fellow countrymen living in the empire content and therefore unwilling to revolt and join their fatherland, these leaders, and numerous citizens as well, had lashed out at Austria, vilifying the empire to try to keep old hatreds alive. As a result, feelings between the two nations were running high by June 1914, and Austrian leaders found it easy to turn their suspicions into outright accusations.

Austrian leaders found it not just easy, but practical as well, to blame Serbia, believing that the assassinations presented an opportunity to take action and put an end to the difficulties with their neighbor once and for all. On July 23, after lengthy discussions and under the pretense of seeking justice, Austrian leaders gave Serbia an ultimatum. These leaders insisted, among other things, that Serbian officials suppress the many anti-Austrian publications and societies in their country, eliminate all anti-Austrian books and teachers from Serbian schools, and dismiss all officials who had promoted anti-Austrian propaganda. In addition, these leaders demanded that Austrian judges oversee the trials—in Serbia—of Princip and the five of his six cohorts who had been arrested. To make sure that Serbia took these orders seriously, Austria announced that if its neighbor did not accept the ultimatum within forty-eight hours, the empire would declare war.

The terms were a bit much for any independent nation to accept. Even so, Serbian officials scrambled to try to keep the peace. Minutes before the deadline expired, officials accepted most of the ultimatum, then suggested that the rest, especially the issue of Austrian judges sitting in Serbia, be put before mediators from other nations to sort out. The empire refused to accept any intervention; instead it declared war on July 28.

When a bitter war between France and Germany finally ended in 1871, Germany, the victor, tried to eliminate the threat of French retaliation by becoming so strong that France—or any other enemy—would realize that an assault would be futile. To do this, German leaders sought allies who would help Germany if attacked. In return, it promised to do likewise for its partners. Not to be outdone or outflanked, France also sought allies. Both sides were successful, and as a result, Europe by 1914 was divided into two powerful, hostile camps.

One of Germany's allies was Austria. After the assassinations, Germany's leader, Kaiser Wilhelm II, encouraged the Austrians to punish—and therefore weaken—their neighbor, because the kaiser believed that even though troops had not actually marched into Austria, it had been attacked, and more important, Serbia's ambition to unite all Serbs was a threat to the stability of Central Europe. To show his support for Austria, Wilhelm II promised his ally unlimited military assistance if war should occur.

Meanwhile, Russia, ruled by Czar Nicholas II, prepared to help its friend, Serbia. Russia sent soldiers to the German border, where the heavily armed men were poised for an invasion at a moment's notice if Germany declared war on Serbia. Not surprisingly, Germany considered the presence of troops on its border threatening, and German leaders demanded that Russia withdraw its men. When the czar refused to do so, Germany declared war on Russia on August 1.

Russia's allies included France and Great Britain. Believing that these countries would help Russia, which would force Germany to fight on two fronts at the same time, Germany's military leaders decided to invade and conquer France before it had a chance to mobilize for all-out war or provide a foothold on the continent for British troops. These military leaders unrealistically planned to defeat France in a week, two at the most.

The French-German border had been heavily fortified after the war between the two nations ended in 1871. As a result, the easiest way for German troops to invade France was through Belgium. So German leaders sought permission to march through this tiny country. Belgian officials quickly and forcefully reminded German leaders that Belgium was a neutral nation, not a road, and as such it could not permit any foreign soldiers to pass through to attack another country. Belgian officials then produced the treaty the two nations had signed more than eighty years before respecting Belgium's neutrality and insisted that Germany live up to its promises.

Unwilling to give up on the easy route and eager to attack France as quickly as possible, Germany's leaders simply ignored the treaty. They ordered German soldiers into Belgium and then France. On August 4, while French troops were rushing to the front lines to meet their enemy on what became known as the Western Front, Great Britain declared war on Germany.

In the coming months and years, the number of countries involved in the war would soar to thirty-two. Germany, Austria-Hungary, and their two allies, Bulgaria and the Ottoman Empire, were called the Central Powers. Russia, France, Great Britain, and their supporters, twenty-eight in all, were referred to as the Allied Powers, or more often, simply the Allies.

Although European leaders claimed to have great faith in their alliances, most of them had spent a lot of time and money building up their military forces in the late 1800s and early 1900s. These leaders had militarized for two reasons. First, they didn't trust their allies, some of whom were old enemies. Would they *really* come to one's aid in a crisis? leaders had asked. Second, the late 1800s had been a time of great industrial expansion, and nations had aggressively sought sites that could supply raw materials for manufacturers. Some European countries had actually seized land rich in minerals in both Asia and Africa. Staking out these claims and defending them from rival nations or angry native inhabitants could only be accomplished by countries that had powerful armies and navies. So these empire builders had worked diligently to build the mightiest military forces on earth.

When one country had noticed another building up its forces, especially an old enemy, it had followed suit, encouraging its industries to develop and refine deadly weapons. One of these was the machine gun. It was so efficient at killing that it would force armies to find a new way to defend themselves: an elaborate system of trenches 5 feet (1.5 meters) deep in the ground, which permitted troops to move about out of their enemies' gun sights. Other inventions included tanks, U-boats (underwater boats or submarines), and the most frightening invention of all, poison gas, which when inhaled, could cause a slow, agonizing death.

In short, when war came, alliances dragged many countries into the conflict, each driven by old hatreds and rivalries and armed with stockpiles of weapons of mass destruction. And as a result, more than 30 million people would become casualties in the four-year-long catastrophe, the likes of which the world had not seen before.

At first Americans thought that they could remain neutral in what was then called the Great War. (Today the conflict is more commonly known as World War I. This term was not generally used until another great war, one involving many nations, now called World War II, erupted in 1939.) After all, the fighting was thousands of miles away. Besides, there was a question about which side to support if the United States entered the conflict. More than 8 million Americans traced their ancestry to Germany, and many of them supported the Central Powers. Irish-Americans, 4 million strong, many of whom had chaffed under British rule in their homeland, also supported the Central Powers. Other Americans recalled long-standing ties with Great Britain and France, and they cheered for the Allies. But as the war dragged on, the American public became overwhelmingly sympathetic toward the Allies. This was due in large part to Germany's U-boat warfare and a certain telegram.

Because the United States was neutral, the federal government could not make loans; nor could it furnish supplies to any of the warring nations. However, banks and private businesses could, and they provided money and goods to any nation seeking them.

In order to prevent supplies from reaching their enemies, the British placed mines (explosives) in the North Sea and routinely checked American ships for war matériel bound for Germany, which by international law the Allies had a right to seize. This upset Americans and put a serious strain on the relationship between the United States and Great Britain.

Shortly after, Germany decided to cut supplies going to the Allies by announcing that it was going to conduct all-out submarine warfare, and *any* ship sailing to or from its enemies was considered fair game. This so shocked and enraged Americans that they forgave the British for mining the North Sea.

Not certain that the Germans really meant what they said, Americans continued to ship goods to the Allies, and citizens sailed to England on luxury liners. Intent upon keeping their word, German sailors sank the *Falaba*, a British liner, taking one American to his death on March 28, 1915. While this was alarming, it did not produce outrage in America. However, the next attack did. On May 7, 1915, a German U-boat fired at the *Lusitania*, a British liner carrying more than 1,900 passengers. It sank in less than twenty minutes, taking more than 1,100 passengers to their deaths. Among the dead were 128 Americans, mostly women and children.

Americans were appalled that such a thing could happen. By international law, any ship planning to attack another was supposed to give a warning so that crew members on the targeted vessel might abandon it to save their lives. In this case not only was no warning given, but the target was a liner, which was unable

Irish soldiers and sailors pay their respects at a common grave for a number of victims of the Lusitania *sinking by a German U-boat.*

to protect itself, and its passengers were civilians, not military personnel. Americans demonstrated, showing both their sorrow and anger, and some demanded that the United States enter the war and teach Germany a lesson it would never forget.

But President Wilson was determined to keep the United States out of the conflict. Instead of asking Congress to declare war, Wilson exchanged harsh words with German leaders, who eventually promised to give all ships a warning in the future.

For more than a year, America struggled to maintain its neutrality. Then in January 1917, Germany, believing that victory was within reach if it took a daring step, announced that it would once again sink any ship headed for British ports. German military officers knew that the British were desperately short of foodstuffs, and they believed that if all supplies could be cut off, Great Britain could be forced to surrender before America could fully mobilize for battle. On February 1, when U-boat warfare resumed, the United States broke diplomatic relations with Germany. However, America still did not declare war.

But in March three events changed America's position. Early that month British officials gave U.S. leaders a copy of a telegram that they had intercepted. This message had been sent on February 24 to the German ambassador in Mexico by Alfred Zimmermann, the German foreign minister. In the telegram, the ambassador was told to encourage the Mexican government, which at the time had a strained relationship with the United States, to enter the conflict if America declared war on Germany. In exchange for joining the Central Powers and forcing the United States to fight on two fronts, Zimmermann had promised Mexico significant spoils of war, including land in New Mexico, Texas, and Arizona. This angered Americans, especially those living in the states that were to be turned over to Mexico, moving them one step closer to war.

A few days later, in part because of the huge losses suffered in the war, the Russian people revolted, and they forced their czar to step down. On March 12, Russian leaders laid the groundwork for a new government. Czar Nicholas II had been a cruel ruler, and many American leaders had resisted entering the war on the same side as Russia because they didn't want to be an ally of the Russian crown. But now with Nicholas II out of power, America would be fighting only with democracies, making the declaration of war all the more likely.

On March 16 the United States was given yet another reason for declaring war. German U-boats sank three American merchant ships, the *City of Memphis*, the *Illinois*, and the *Valencia*. American patience was now at an end.

So on April 2, 1917, in one of his most famous speeches, President Woodrow Wilson asked Congress for a declaration of war against Germany. Before the hushed crowd of legislators and guests, he reviewed all the events that had led to this moment: Germany's invasion of Belgium; the loss of American life at sea, the result of U-boat warfare; and the ruthless determination of the kaiser to conquer his neighbors, which he said, was now a threat to all democracies. He concluded by saying:

> There are, it may be, many months of fiery trials and sacrifice ahead of us. It is a fearful thing to lead this great peaceful people into war, into the most terrible and disastrous of all wars, civilization itself seeming to be in the balance. But the right is more precious than peace, and we shall fight for the things which we have always carried nearest our hearts . . . and to make the world itself at last free. To such a task we can dedicate our lives and our fortunes, everything that we are and everything that we have, with the pride of those who know that the day has come when America is privileged to spend her blood and her might for the principles that gave her birth and happiness and the peace which she has treasured. God helping her, she can do no other.[1]

In the days that followed, legislators debated the president's request. On April 4 the Senate voted for a declaration of war, 82–6. The House of Representatives did likewise, 373–50, on April 6.

Although all who voted against entering the conflict received attention from their colleagues and then the public, few received as much scrutiny as Representative Jeannette Rankin did. Sworn into office on April 6, she was the first woman to be elected to Congress and the only woman to have a voice in this decision. When Rankin did not say "aye" or "nay" on the first vote, knowing full well she would be given a second chance to announce her decision, one of the most powerful representatives in Congress, Joe Cannon, approached her desk to give her some advice. Believing that Rankin might abstain altogether,

Cannon said, "Little woman, you cannot afford not to vote. You represent the womanhood of the country in the American Congress."[2]

The second time Rankin's name was called, all eyes in the chamber turned toward her. She rose slowly, then said in a voice strained by emotion, "I want to stand by my country, but I cannot vote for war. I vote no."[3] Immediately eyebrows all over the House shot up. Many shared Cannon's view, believing that Rankin spoke for all women. Now representatives wondered if women would support this war, and if so, what role they would play. What role indeed?

CHAPTER TWO

Which *SIDE* ARE YOU ON?

> *As women we are particularly charged with the future of child-hood and with the care of the helpless and the unfortunate. We will no longer endure without protest that added burden of maimed and invalid men and poverty-stricken widows and orphans which was placed upon us [in past wars]. . . . We demand that women be given a share in deciding between war and peace.*
>
> Woman's Peace Party

When Jeannette Rankin cast her vote against America's entry into World War I, she symbolized the dramatic changes that had taken place in women's lives since America's earliest days. These changes helped determine the unique roles women would play in this war.

During the colonial period, a woman's place was thought to be the home. There, according to most—but not all—colonists, frail females could use their natural, God-given talents for cooking, cleaning, and raising children. By remaining at home, women could also be protected from the corruption of the outside world. This was important because women, who were thought to be purer in spirit than men, were responsible for the morals of their children.

But when a war erupted and American leaders realized that women could and would provide vital aid, women's roles expanded. This was especially true during the Civil War (1861–1865), when necessity forced some Northern and Southern manufacturers and government officials to hire female workers.

To make the idea of women in the workplace acceptable to the public, at least for the duration of the Civil War, employers argued that the tasks the women would be doing were nothing more than an extension of what they had always done at home. For generations, employers argued, women had made clothing for their families. Why shouldn't they make uniforms for soldiers? Since women supposedly thrived on neatness and repetition, two requirements of good housekeeping, why shouldn't they be hired to keep records and file letters in the government's offices? And because women had been responsible for the health of their families, why couldn't they care for wounded soldiers? So women were encouraged to work for pay outside their homes during the conflict, and those who had chaffed at their previously limited lifestyle sought work with enthusiasm.

When the war was over, women were expected to return to their former roles. However, for many this was impossible. The long, bloody conflict had claimed the lives of more than 600,000 men and had disabled several hundred thousand more. This tragic loss not only brought grief to the soldiers' loved ones, but it also forced many widows and wives to find ways to support their families. In addition, the massive loss of life on the battlefield meant that 30 percent—instead of the usual 10 percent—of young women would not marry due to the dearth of eligible males. These women would also have to find some way to provide for themselves. And finally, many of the approximately 4 million slaves set free were women, and they, too, had to support themselves, and in many cases, some family members as well.

Not only did many women's lives forever change after the Civil War, so did America as it became more and more industrialized. Thriving manufacturing firms provided more employment opportunities than ever before, though most paid very low wages. Even so, many Americans abandoned their farms and villages to seek jobs in the cities, believing that industry eventually could provide a better future. These workers were joined by millions of immigrants, first from countries such as Germany and Ireland, and later from nations such as Italy, Poland, Serbia, and Russia.

Although almost all industries would hire male workers, women were primarily employed in textile mills and garment manufacturing firms. In fact, these

Down on the Farm

It was no wonder that Americans abandoned the countryside for jobs in the cities in the early 1900s. Running a farm was hard work, requiring the help of every member of the family, including farm wives, who at the turn of the century made up the majority of working women in America. Well aware of the burden that farm women were carrying, in early 1914 the U.S. Department of Agriculture sent questionnaires to these women to try to determine how best to help them. Many wives included letters with their responses. Below is an excerpt from one woman's report, whose comments were typical:

> The condition of the farm women of the South is most deplorable. Her liege lord is availing himself of labor-saving appliances such as reaper, binder, thresher, riding plow, gas engines, etc., while the woman's labor-saving help consists of her sewing and washing machines. The routine work of the Southern farm woman is about as follows: at this time of year she is up at 5 A.M. preparing the breakfast, often building her own fire; milks the cows, cares for the milk—churns the cream by hand. Puts the house in order, gets the dinner, eats with the family at noon; leaves the house in disorder, goes to the . . . field. . . . At about sundown she goes to the farmhouse, puts the house in order, washes the dishes left over from the noon meal, prepares the supper—most of the time too tired to eat; gets the children to bed, and falls asleep herself—and so it goes on from day to day. Somehow she finds the time to do the washing, ironing, mending, knitting, and darning between times.[1]

When the United States entered the Great War and millions of marching, fighting American soldiers required more calories than they had as civilians, the demand for food skyrocketed. Then farmers and their wives, including the woman who wrote the report, were expected to do even more.

industries employed more than 1 million of the 5 million females in the labor force in the early 1900s. The vast majority of these workers were under the age of twenty-five, and 75 percent of them were single; it was socially unacceptable for married women to work outside the home, although some were forced to do so out of dire economic necessity.

Mill and garment employees encountered difficult working conditions. Competition was fierce in the marketplace, and as a result employers put little money into their businesses in order to produce as inexpensive a product as possible. Workrooms—commonly called sweatshops even though they were very cold in the winter—usually lacked proper lighting, forcing workers to struggle to see what they were doing. Ventilation also was poor. Dust from piles of fabric as well as fumes from stacks of oily rags used to clean machines fouled the air, presenting both health and safety hazards.

Because employers wanted as many finished products to sell as possible, they had strict work rules. For example, no one could talk while working, and employees were fined if they didn't return from their breaks on time. To make sure that workers didn't take an extra break, supervisors bolted the exits of the workrooms—on the outside. This practice was modified somewhat after a disastrous fire swept through the Triangle Shirtwaist Company in New York City in 1911, and 143 women and 3 men who had been locked inside their workshop died.

Garment workers were usually paid by the piece—that is, the number of collars, sleeves, or cuffs they could finish—and the pressure to produce enough to earn a living caused great stress. Even at top speed, few women earned more than $6 per week for sixty hours of work. Employers justified paying females extremely low wages for two reasons. First, supervisors argued, unlike men who often worked for one company their entire lives, most women were little more than temporary workers, filling time until they married. Second, what women were doing was seldom more than a typical household task, which had always been done for free. When, employers asked, had a female demanded money from her father, brother, or husband for making a shirt for him?

Cities were not equipped to handle the large number of workers arriving daily, so finding housing was a real challenge. To meet the need and earn a lot of money in the process, landlords turned old buildings into as many apartments as possible. As a result, it was not unusual for an entire working-class family—parents, and on average, four children—to live in two or three small rooms.

To help pay the rent, which ran as high as $5 a week, often a third of what many men earned, some wives took in boarders and mothers did piecework at home, enlisting the aid of their children whenever possible. If necessary, sons and daughters thirteen and fourteen years of age, and sometimes even younger, were expected to leave school and seek work to help their parents meet expenses.

Besides being crowded, the buildings, called tenements, had limited facilities. Renters got their water—cold only—from a faucet in the hallway and shared a

Female garment workers of the early twentieth century often toiled in cramped, stuffy spaces and were paid very little for long hours of work.

bathroom with a dozen or more people. Central heat was not common, so most tenants warmed their units with cooking stoves, many of which burned coal, a fuel that coated apartment interiors with soot. Under such conditions, it was difficult for women to keep apartments and children clean, so disease was common.

Although few women in the garment industry—whether in the workshop or doing piecework at home—reaped much benefit from their jobs, most manufacturing concerns produced wealth for their owners and, eventually, rising wages for their male workers. This significantly expanded America's middle class in the late 1800s and early 1900s, creating a comfortable lifestyle for many married women and their daughters that contrasted sharply in at least four ways to that of the young women who toiled in the clothing industry.

First, rising incomes made it possible for middle-class women to hire servants to do the most tedious household tasks. In 1900 the demand for such laborers was so strong and the availability of decent jobs for women so limited that 2 million women worked for pay *in* homes. Most women who took these positions were immigrants or daughters of immigrants who spoke little or no English, or poverty-stricken black women, many of whom were wives and mothers, who, because of racial prejudice, had difficulty finding any meaningful employment.

Second, growing incomes made it possible for middle-class women to buy products that poorer women had to make themselves. Store-bought bread, clothing off the rack or out of a catalog, and canned goods were now readily available to anyone who had the money to buy them. In addition, by the time World War I broke out, 35 percent of American homes, mostly middle-class and wealthy households, had electricity, and family members in these houses could purchase laborsaving devices such as washing machines.

Third, a rising middle class meant that more girls than ever could remain in school rather than being put to work to help support their families. Upon graduation, young women who had taken typing and shorthand classes joined the growing ranks of office workers, 600,000 men and women in the early 1900s. Because secretarial work paid more than the garment industry did and the working environment was clean, many parents considered it an ideal position for their daughters until they married. In 1900, 75 percent of all typists were women, up from less than 3 percent in 1870.

A high-school education also made it possible for young women to join a new and rapidly growing business, the telephone company. At a time when push-button phones were only a dream, all calls had to be completed by an operator. Whenever a subscriber wanted to place a call, he or she picked up the phone, causing a light to go on at one of the telephone company's switchboards. An operator responded by plugging a cable connected to his or her headset into the jack next to the light. This enabled the operator to ask the caller for a number. After receiving instructions, the operator took a cable next to the subscriber's jack and made the requested connection.

Long-distance phone calls were rare, but when they occurred an operator usually had to route a call through several switchboards. Because sound could travel over telephone lines for only 1,000 miles (1,600 kilometers) in the early 1900s, repeaters were stationed in offices along the lines. These people restated an operator's request or a caller's message to the next person.

Women were considered ideal telephone operators and repeaters; their voices were thought to be more pleasant than men's, and the women were regarded as more detail-oriented than male operators. When America entered the war, 99 percent of all operators were women, approximately 88,000 in all.

The fourth difference between working-class and middle-class families was the opportunity for advanced education that money made possible. Middle-class families could send their daughters to college, and these women, upon graduation, could enter the professions. When America entered World War I, more than 700,000 women were employed as teachers, nurses, and social workers. A few had even managed to become full-fledged lawyers, gaining the right to present cases in court. And one, Jeannette Rankin, had been elected to Congress.

At the same time that the United States was becoming industrialized, some Americans were being swept up in the Progressive Movement. Progressives were appalled by many practices of the day, especially those of rich industrialists who often thrived at the expense of their workers. Progressives also were deeply upset with numerous politicians, handpicked by party bosses, who ignored the will of the people as well as the public's needs. Idealistic and highly energetic, progressives rolled up their sleeves, presented their case to any man or woman willing to listen, and set out to reform America.

Among the progressives were many social workers who decided to devote their lives to helping destitute women and children. Some of these workers, such as Jane Addams, started special houses (in Addams's case, Hull House in Chicago) near tenements where women could seek information about nutrition, medical care, and child rearing, and if they were immigrants, learn to speak English.

Social workers were joined by middle-class women, who, after hearing a few progressives speak, thought that America had some serious problems. Better educated than ever before, encouraged by the Progressive Movement to take

Jeannette Rankin (1880–1973)

Jeannette Rankin was born in Missoula, Montana, where she spent her entire childhood. She was deeply interested in helping the poor, and after receiving her bachelor's degree from the University of Montana, enrolled in the New York School for Philanthropy, the forerunner of the Columbia School of Social Work.

Meanwhile, women across the country were fighting for the right to vote. Unable to get Congress to take the issue seriously, suffragists battled for the ballot on a state-by-state basis. Rankin, who found politics fascinating, quickly became involved in the suffrage crusade in Montana. After much prodding, legislators there finally granted women the right to vote in 1914, making Montana the sixth state to do so. (Wyoming, Colorado, Idaho, Utah, and Washington had already given women the ballot.)

Finally able to vote and hold office, Jeannette Rankin decided to run for Congress in 1916. Although her campaign was successful, she lost most of her support in Montana on the same day she entered the House of Representatives. Her vote against America's entry into World War I on April 6 enraged many Montanans. The *Helena Independent* spoke for them when the editor called Rankin "a dupe of the Kaiser" and, because she had shown emotion when she cast her vote, "a crying schoolgirl" as well.[2]

Strong feelings against Rankin did not die down during her two-year term, and as a result, she lost her bid for reelection in 1918. In fact, she would not win reelection until 1940. She was a member of the House when President Franklin D. Roosevelt asked for a declaration of war against Japan after it bombed Pearl Harbor on December 7, 1941. True to her pacifist beliefs, Rankin refused to support the president's request, making her the only person in U.S. history to vote against entering both world wars.

Jeannette Rankin in 1918, with the Capitol in the background

action, and having time to devote to social causes thanks to the help of servants at home, thousands of these women set out with determination to clean up tenements, protect children, and give some of their working-class sisters a helping hand. Whenever critics questioned the women's involvement in public affairs, women said that they simply had expanded their traditional roles to include a new kind of tidying up. They called it "civic housekeeping."

Their housekeeping was effective. In the years leading up to World War I, middle-class women helped establish a hundred Hull Houses, petitioned for—and won—inspection of the textile and garment industries, and spearheaded drives for legislation to outlaw child labor. These women also marched on picket lines when textile workers, who were becoming feisty, successfully went on strike for better wages and working conditions. (However, middle-class women did not support servants when *they* threatened to strike.) Although the reformers accomplished many goals, they felt that they would be even more effective if all women could vote, so they also renewed their drive to gain suffrage with vigor.

When war erupted in Europe in 1914, women like Jane Addams, heady from the successes they had experienced, decided to expand their role even further. In 1915, Addams and delegates from many women's organizations formed the Woman's Peace Party. Believing that America's entry into the war was all but certain if the conflict dragged on, party members argued that they were doing little more than extending their domestic role once again. They had, they pointed out, always been responsible for caring for widows, orphans, and wounded soldiers, and recalling their grandmothers' experiences in the Civil War, these modern-day women weren't eager to carry such a burden. Therefore, they hoped to appeal to reason and encourage a negotiated settlement. Representatives from the Woman's Peace Party met with female delegates from the Central Powers in Europe in 1915, but despite their best efforts on all sides, military leaders refused to take the women's pleas for settlement seriously.

When America entered the conflict, women had to decide if they would support the war. Some, like Jeannette Rankin, were pacifists who believed that fighting was morally wrong and a terrible waste of lives. These women pointed to the horrendous losses on the battlefields—France had suffered more than a million casualties in one year—and insisted that lives were better spent improving working conditions in textile mills and living conditions in tenements.

Carrie Chapman Catt (1859–1947)

Carrie Chapman Catt, one of the most influential and best-known suffragists in U.S. history, supported America's entry into World War I. Unlike Jeannette Rankin, she believed that it was the patriotic duty of all women to do so. Also, she feared that if women did not back the war effort, their lack of enthusiasm would be held against them, seriously damaging their effort to secure the ballot.

Catt, born Carrie Lane, spent most of her youth in Iowa. After graduation from high school—in three years—she decided to attend college. Because her father could not pay for her education, she took a teaching position to earn money for her tuition. (Unlike today, high-school graduates then could teach if they passed rigorous examinations.) In 1877 she entered Iowa State College at Ames, where, after receiving her degree, she hoped to study law.

Needing money for tuition, Carrie again went to work, becoming a school principal in Mason City, Iowa. There she met Leo Chapman, the local newspaper editor-publisher. They were married in 1885.

Mrs. Chapman became her husband's assistant editor. At the time, women in Iowa were just beginning to press for suffrage. After writing several articles about this issue, Carrie joined the crusade for the ballot, which was unsuccessful then, circulating petitions and giving speeches. A few months later, Leo Chapman died, leaving a brokenhearted widow who vowed that she would never again marry. Instead, she would devote her life to the suffrage cause.

However, five years later George Catt persuaded Carrie to become his wife. A strong supporter of women's rights, Mr. Catt argued that they would make a fine team. He would earn a large income for them (he was a successful engineer who built bridges), and she could do the couple's public service by continuing her fight for the ballot. Her marriage to Catt, which was a happy one, made it financially possible for Carrie to travel all over America, giving speeches and raising funds. In the process, she built a name for herself. In 1900 she was elected president of the National American Woman Suffrage Association.

When America declared war, leaders of the association quickly announced that their organization would support the war effort. Mrs. Catt even went so far as to volunteer the association's members for the armed forces, an offer that must have made military leaders smile, for many of the suffragists were older women.

At the same time, Carrie Chapman Catt made it perfectly clear that while the association would encourage members to perform every war-related task that came their way, the association wasn't about to put its demand for the vote on hold. She pointed to the irony that the United States was willing to go to war to protect democracy abroad while denying women at home the most basic democratic right, the right to vote. Catt argued that women would serve more willingly if they could vote, and therefore, it would be a clever, not to mention downright decent, decision on the part of Congress and the states to give women the ballot.

Although her demand was not met immediately, Catt's goal, for which she had fought for more than thirty years, would soon be realized.

Pacifists were joined by progressives and socialists. Progressives were opposed to this war because they feared that the progress being made on the social issues that were so dear to their hearts would come to a sudden halt if the country geared up for a massive military drive. Socialists argued that the poor fought wars for the benefit of the rich, especially industrialists who manufactured weapons.

While some reformers saw the war as a serious threat to their goals, others saw this war as an opportunity to further their causes and turn the whole world into a better place in which to live. President Wilson's pledge to make the world safe for democracy and the belief that this would be the war to end all wars since the world's tyrants would be soundly defeated especially appealed to these women. So they wholeheartedly offered their support.

These crusaders were joined by millions of women, who, as they watched their sons, brothers, and sweethearts march off to war, used their skills as industrial workers, typists, telephone operators, nurses, doctors, social workers, and volunteers to help the men. In so doing, they provided invaluable aid and could rightly claim a role in the victory that was finally achieved. At the same time, unlike in past wars, many women, including some who did not support the war, hardened by years of toiling in industry and emboldened by gains they had made in treating some of society's ills, demanded fair treatment for women on the home front. In doing this, they greatly expanded women's rights and roles during a difficult time. This was no small achievement, even for the extraordinary women of World War I.

CHAPTER THREE

Wanted: WOMEN WORKERS

*All the colored women like [our work for the railroad] and want
to keep it. We are making more money at this than any work we
can get [$3 per day], and we do not have to work as hard as at
housework which requires us to be on duty from six o'clock in the
morning until nine or ten at night, with might little time off and
at very poor wages.*

Helen Ross, Santa Fe Railroad employee

Waging all-out war in 1914 was expensive. Armies on both sides needed millions of uniforms, warm jackets, leather boots, helmets, eating utensils, cots, blankets, tents, guns, bullets in unlimited numbers, literally tons of food each day, ships, tanks, and a few airplanes.

To make it financially possible for the Central Powers and the Allies to buy supplies from American industries when the fighting started, American banks loaned large sums of money to both sides. Bankers raised this money by selling war bonds to the public. These bonds, which were really loans from individuals (holders received the money they paid for their bonds plus interest at a specified time), gave people a chance to earn a little money and support the side of their choice. Bonds were popular, eventually garnering more than 2 million dollars for the Central Powers and 2 billion dollars for the Allies.

As orders from foreign nations soared—shipments abroad increased as much as 35 percent in one year alone, in large part due to the demand for food and weapons—farmers and manufacturers alike looked about for more workers. But the usual source of cheap labor, a million immigrants who had come to America each year, ended when war broke out in Europe. In addition, most men of working age already were gainfully employed. Many manufacturers had little choice then but to hire a few women.

When the United States declared war in 1917 and 4 million young men were drafted for the armed services, America's labor shortage became serious. In addition to requests from the Allies (it was now illegal to sell anything to the Central Powers), orders from the federal government for war matériel poured into U.S. industries. However, many of these orders could not be filled until more workers could be found. As a result, manufacturers now actively sought female employees. So gutsy women, eager to support the war effort and equally eager to find a decent job, applied for nontraditional positions. These workers were more than willing to operate drills, milling machines, turret lathes, grinders, and welding tools.

Although many industrialists wanted to hire women, most male employees were staunchly opposed to this, war or no war. The men's resistance was due primarily to the fact that women had been willing to work for low wages in the past, and men believed—and employers hoped—that women would continue to do so. Male workers thought that this would result in lowering their own incomes, for if enough women were available, employers could demand that men take a pay cut or be replaced.

This notion was not new; for years men believed that women in the workplace would cause wages to plummet. However, this was not a serious problem for male employees as long as women were confined to entry-level positions in the garment and textile industries, where few men worked. But when some women began to take nontraditional jobs in the late 1800s, male workers panicked. Although they were not able to stop employers from hiring women, worried men were capable of making female laborers feel unwelcome. Some men refused to work beside women, let alone train them, while others prohibited females from becoming union members. This limited the women's ability to voice their concerns about working conditions, since all issues traditionally went through union representatives.

Women capably stepped into factory jobs that had been previously held by men, such as tire finishing (above) and pharmaceuticals (below).

Refusing to be stymied by the men's hostility and realizing the value of banding together, women started unions of their own. By 1903 membership was so strong that union leaders were able to form an umbrella organization to unite all women's unions, the Women's Trade Union League (WTUL). Membership was open to all working men and women, even if they didn't belong to a union, suffragists, and members of various reform groups. By 1915 the WTUL was raising money, often from middle-class and wealthy members, to pay the salaries of union organizers. These organizers worked hard, dramatically increasing the number of female union members—300,000 strong in 1917—and the clout of the WTUL as well.

On June 9, 1917, the WTUL held a meeting in Kansas City, Missouri. Fearful that women, in their zeal to support the war, would undermine progress made in the workplace, such as safer working conditions, delegates devised a list of standards that the WTUL expected Congress to adopt and any employer accepting government contracts to follow. In exchange, the WTUL would encourage all women to support the war effort, either as workers or volunteers.

The women's demands were straightforward. First, the delegates said, children belonged in school. So no matter how serious the labor shortage was, no industry was to hire children under the age of fourteen. Second, no industry was to assign piecework to tenement women, where working conditions and pay could not be monitored. Third, female workers would not work for a pittance. Not only did the WTUL expect manufacturers to pay females a fair wage, the WTUL expected employers to pay women the same wage that men received if they were doing the same job. And fourth, industries that hired women were to be inspected regularly to make sure that they were providing safe working conditions. Furthermore, inspecting teams were to include females, delegates said, since they were better qualified than men to decide what was and what wasn't a threat to a woman's health.

Needing the support of women to win the war, the government accepted the WTUL's demands. In fact, not only would women serve as inspectors, but some, such as suffragist Carrie Chapman Catt, would also be assigned to various boards that were coordinating the war effort. Women were overjoyed at their sudden rise to prominence. However, they quickly learned that all was not exactly as it seemed.

One of the women chosen to be an inspector was Mary Anderson. Anderson had immigrated from Sweden to America's Midwest along with an older sister in 1889 when Mary was sixteen years old. Until she could speak English, Anderson had a job as a dishwasher in a hotel. Later she became a stitcher in a large shoe factory in Chicago, where she joined the International Boot and Shoe Workers Union and the WTUL. When America entered the war, Anderson, because of her work experience and her involvement in the WTUL, was asked by government leaders to head the Women in Industry Service, a council that regulated the working conditions of women in wartime industries, a position she quickly accepted.

One of Anderson's responsibilities was to inspect various workplaces. But even with the power of the federal government behind her, she encountered many obstacles while doing so. Anderson later recalled:

> I remember going to Bridgeport [Connecticut] with a group of several men and one other woman to inspect some factories. . . . The group never got into a factory. . . . Day after day [our guide] put us off saying the management was "about" ready to let us in. After nearly a week of waiting we left in disgust.[1]

Although inspectors fretted about unsafe working conditions and unfair wages, many industries, especially those run by the federal government during the war, really tried to be fair to all workers. As a result, many women earned high wages for the first time in their lives. A female streetcar conductor was typical of these women. She said:

> Lightest work I ever did and best pay. Have worked at housework, done clerical work, and [worked] as a telephone operator. Had to do heavy lifting when I checked orders in the drug company; filled a man's place at $15.00 a week, while men beside me got twice that. Do you wonder I appreciate being treated as well and paid just the same as a man?[2]

Because it was socially unacceptable for married women to work outside the home, the supply of female workers was limited. Only a million women joined the workforce from 1915 to 1918, and many of these did not produce war matériel. Instead, most of the war-related jobs went to women already in the workforce. These experienced workers, many of whom came from the garment industry, applied for industrial positions as soon as they were available. Jobs in the garment and textile mills were then claimed by servants or young women new to the workplace.

As servants took new jobs, middle-class and wealthy families struggled to find someone to cook their meals, clean their homes, and do their laundry. Also, manufacturers, a number of which had expanded during the war, needed someone to clean their buildings. So employers teamed up to bring black women working in homes or fields in the South, where wages were very low, to the North. More than 500,000 blacks relocated during the war, and many of these were women seeking better jobs. A cook or a laundress could make as much in a day in the North as she could in a week in the South. Women who were hired by the railroads to clean passenger cars made even more.

The desire to go North, called "Northern fever," swept through whole Southern communities. One black woman in Mississippi said, "Every time I go home I have to pass house after house of all my friends who are in the North and are prospering." She thought that she might "go wild" if she stayed in Mississippi much longer.[3]

If an industry had segregated facilities—in general, blacks and whites did not work or live side by side in the early 1900s—employers sometimes hired former black servants. Even though they never accounted for more than 7 percent of the female workforce in industry, these women made significant contributions to the war effort, taking on some of the least desirable jobs, such as scrubbing fruits and vegetables for canning and making explosives.

As pleas for workers increased, so did wages in war-related businesses. Even secretaries and telephone operators began to leave their offices for jobs in industry. By the end of the war, women accounted for 20 percent of the workforce in the airplane, leather, and food industries.

Because the demand for workers was so great, some employers feared that their workers might look for better jobs. In order to keep women from doing this, supervisors stressed the significant contribution the women were making to the war effort. As the supervisors did so, female workers gained considerable self-esteem along with experience and skills. No longer limited to sweatshops, they and the leaders of the WTUL eyed the outcome of the war and their future with confidence. And they had every reason to do so. One of the WTUL's leaders said, almost in awe of what had been accomplished: "At last, after centuries of . . . discrimination, women are coming into the labor and festival of life on equal terms with men."[4] It was a new role for women, and it was welcomed by many.

CHAPTER FOUR

YEOMANETTES and MORE

Before and [during the battle at St. Mihiel] we were rushed to death; we worked day and night. The strain was pretty bad; offi-cers were all on edge, and it was rather hard to keep our tempers at times because everything came at once. . . . The [telephone] lines would go out of order [because of] bombs and thunder-storms.

Esther Fresnel, telephone operator, Army Signal Corps

In early March 1917, Secretary of the Navy Josephus Daniels was deeply trou-bled. Convinced, correctly, that the United States would declare war shortly and well aware that he would need thousands of typists and clerks to prepare orders and keep records for all the men who would be recruited, he worried aloud about where he would find the necessary personnel. Because women were now leaving offices for better wages in industry, he knew that the Civil Service, which had provided secretaries for the military in the past, couldn't find enough cler-ical workers to staff the government's offices. How, he wondered, could the service possibly provide the large number of workers the military would require? Training male recruits to type and file appeared to be the only solution, but this would take months to accomplish, and Daniels wasn't sure that he had that much time.

GEE !!
I WISH I WERE
A MAN

I'd JOIN
The NAVY

Howard Chandler Christy. 1915

BE A MAN AND DO IT
UNITED STATES NAVY
RECRUITING STATION

Women soon found that they didn't have to be men to serve their country in the Navy or other branches of the armed services. This poster, by artist Howard Chandler Christy, dates from 1917.

After pondering the question for a few days, Daniels stunned his aides by asking, "Is there any regulation which specifies that a Navy yeoman be a man?" When wide-eyed aides indicated that although it was assumed that only men would serve in the military, the Navy's regulations did not state that yeomen (recruits) had to be male. "Then enroll women in the Naval Reserve as yeomen," Daniels said, "and we will have the best clerical assistance the country can provide."[1]

Secretary Daniels may have thought that this would solve the problem, but a number of men serving under him did not. They thought that enlisting women—who were regarded as too timid or too bossy, depending upon who was doing the describing—would be a disaster. Legal advisors in the Navy were among the loudest naysayers. Fearing that women would soon be assigned to their offices, they shouted, "Petticoats in the Navy! Damn'd outrage! Helluva mess! Back to sea f'r me!"[2]

Although Daniels's decision caused a ruckus, he went ahead with his plan. On March 19, he authorized recruiting agents to accept women for secretarial positions. To encourage women to sign up, Daniels promised female recruits wages equal to those of male clerks, which were higher than most businesses paid, and because there were no rooms in the barracks suitable for women, an allowance for housing as well. Enlistees would also receive an allotment for smart uniforms, which were being cut and stitched at that very moment.

The Navy established high standards for female recruits to make sure that the program didn't fail. Would-be enlistees had to be between the ages of eighteen and thirty-five, have a high-school education (a college degree was even better), be of good character, and have a neat appearance. In addition, women had to pass stiff typing, shorthand, and spelling tests. As a result, by April 6, the same day the House voted to declare war, although more than a thousand women had applied, only two hundred had been accepted.

Once war was declared, Daniels appealed to women's patriotism to provide a larger pool of volunteers to select from, arguing that women not only could actually participate in the defeat of the Central Powers by joining the Navy, but also that each volunteer could free up a man to fight. The secretary's plea was successful; eventually more than 11,000 women enlisted, serving in naval offices all over America.

Joy Bright Hancock (1898–1986)

Joy Bright Hancock has been called the First Lady of the Navy. Born and raised in New Jersey, Joy Bright was attending secretarial school in Philadelphia when Secretary Josephus Daniels decided to enlist women in the Naval Reserve. Bright immediately applied, and shortly after, she began to work for a construction firm in Camden, New Jersey, that made ships for the Navy. Not only was she one of the first yeomanettes, a likeness of her was used on posters during the war, making her one of the best-known volunteers.

When victory was declared, Bright wanted to remain in the reserve. Unable to do so—all women were sent packing at war's end—Bright secured a position in the corps as a civilian. She left this post in 1924 when she married Lieutenant Commander Lewis Hancock.

When the United States entered World War II in 1941, Joy Bright Hancock joined the Navy's WAVES (Women Accepted for Volunteer Emergency Service). She was one of only two women in the Navy who could wear a victory ribbon on her uniform, a decoration indicating that the wearer had served in World War I. (Eunice White was the other former yeomanette who volunteered for the WAVES.) Bright moved through the ranks rapidly during the war. As a leader, she worked hard to make the best use of the WAVES' skills both to support the war effort and to give women an opportunity to shine.

After World War II ended, Hancock successfully lobbied for the permanent acceptance of women in the Navy. In 1946 she became the director of the WAVES and later achieved the coveted rank of captain. Until she retired in 1953, Captain Hancock worked to expand women's opportunities in the Navy. This was no small task, for many men in the military believed that women did not belong in the armed services. Today the Joy Bright Hancock Award, given annually, is presented to a woman in the Navy who has shown exceptional leadership skills, a woman like the First Lady of the Navy.

Joy Bright in 1918

While young women were volunteering, some Americans were questioning female enlistment. Even though women in large numbers no longer worked only in their home, some Americans still thought that was where women belonged so that they could be protected from the unseemly side of life. When critics ranked employment sites outside the home, they decided that the garment industry was unhealthy, the office was suspect, and the Navy was unacceptable. It had thousands of men, some of whom, faultfinders said, were not gentlemen. Why would a lady *want* to work with them? Some critics actually compared the first volunteers to camp followers, who, in previous wars, cooked for soldiers before the armed services provided meals, took in laundry, or sold tobacco and coffee to the troops. Some followers, those most remembered by the public, had been prostitutes, and now some citizens thought that the yeomanettes, as they were called, were also women of easy virtue.

These slurs, along with images of women in uniform swabbing decks, which weren't accurate either, made it difficult for some parents to accept their daughters' enlistment. Estelle Kemper, who signed on and reported for work the same day, called her family that evening. "My father answered the phone," she said, recalling the day, "and I told him proudly that I had joined the Navy. . . . He gulped and said quickly, 'I'll call your mother.' When I repeated my announcement to her, she was stunned into silence for a moment, then asked weakly, 'Oh, [Estelle], can you ever get out?'" [3]

Recruits like Estelle often worked ten hours a day, six days a week, in the process earning respect for their skills and commitment. These women proved so diligent and resourceful that as soon as nontraditional openings occurred in the Navy, officers enlisted women to work as translators, switchboard electricians, and recruiters.

The Marines also needed clerical workers. However, they made do with male typists until the Marine Corps experienced devastating losses in France in early 1918, and every available man was needed on the battlefield. Major General George Barnett then asked Secretary Daniels, who was also the head of the Marines, for permission to enroll women for clerical duty, which Daniels quickly granted.

Whether the first woman to sign up, Opha Mae Johnson, was the first female to join the corps is questionable. Long before, Lucy Brewer claimed to have served as a Marine aboard the U.S.S. *Constitution* in the War of 1812.

Brewer later wrote a book, *The Female Marine*, about her many experiences, one of which was donning men's clothing to hide her true identity. Some historians believe that Brewer made up the story; others believe that she was indeed the first woman Marine. In either case, by the end of World War I, more than three hundred women had definitely served in the corps—in skirts, not men's clothing.

The Coast Guard also followed the Navy's example. However, the Guard, which was much smaller than the Navy, enrolled fewer than fifty women.

The Army needed clerical workers, too, so Army officials asked Secretary of War Newton Baker who had the final word on Army matters, for permission to enlist women. The secretary referred to the laws regarding Army enlistment that, unlike the Navy's requirements, said that only men could be enrolled. So when the Army's quartermaster general asked for five thousand female secretaries, Secretary Baker sent five thousand men instead. When General John J. Pershing, the commander of American troops, which were known as the American Expeditionary Force (AEF), applied for female clerks, his request was also denied. Pershing, unwilling to give up on freeing his men for duty at the front, borrowed female secretaries from British forces, which had enlisted women in their armed services.

The next time General Pershing decided that he had to have female workers, he didn't bother to ask for permission to enroll them. Instead, because the Army Signal Corps had hired civilians in the past, some of whom were women, Pershing instructed the Corps to find women to work as telephone operators in France. Because Pershing assumed that they would be hired as civilians, not taken on as recruits and therefore not part of the Army, he believed that this wouldn't be a problem.

The new operators would be responsible for connecting soldiers at the front with their commanders at headquarters via telephone lines—a first in American history. These women would also connect American commanders with French generals, whose responses the women would translate. This meant that the women not only had to be experienced operators, but they also had to speak French fluently; a single mistake in a translation could be costly. In addition, because the conversations the operators would hear were highly sensitive, especially those involving future attacks, the women accepted could not have any ties to the Central Powers.

American telephone operators work near the front at Tours, France, in 1918.

This time the War Department, well aware of the need for experienced operators near the battlefield and acknowledging the loophole in the law that made it possible for the corps to hire women, did not object. In fact, the department helped recruit the operators, running ads in many newspapers all over the United States.

More than 7,000 women volunteered for the Signal Corps; approximately 400 were accepted. Some of these volunteers were put on a reserve list, while 250 were immediately assigned to six units and sent to training centers where they sharpened their operating skills and learned Army terminology.

The First Unit had thirty-three women. It was under the command of Grace Banker, a former trainer for the American Telephone and Telegraph Company. On March 1, 1918, this unit set sail for Europe. After the women reached England, they boarded a ferry to cross the English Channel. Dense fog made it impossible for the vessel to move once it was a few miles from shore, so it dropped anchor and waited for the haze to lift. Meanwhile the ferry was an easy target for the Germans, who had a record of sinking one out of every four vessels leaving England's shores. So to be able to abandon ship at a moment's notice, the women stayed on deck for two days and nights. Despite their discomfort and the potential danger they faced, the operators, who were known as "Hello girls," did not complain. Later, Grace Banker, recalled: "What good sports the girls were in that First Unit! They took everything in their stride. They were the pioneers."[4]

These women were followed shortly by five more units. Most of the operators, now a total of 233, worked in offices in Paris or Tours or in Pershing's headquarters in Chaumont.

The telephone lines had to be in operation twenty-four hours a day, seven days a week. Women worked the day shift, while male officers operated the switchboards at night. However, if a major attack was in progress, everyone worked around the clock, four hours on, four hours off, day after day if necessary.

Shortly after the last operator arrived in France in September 1918, Pershing decided to make an assault at St. Mihiel. Because the success of this attack would be crucial to the outcome of the war, General Pershing wanted the best operators possible to accompany the troops. Shortly after, Grace Banker, who selected the operators, Suzanne Prevot, Esther Fresnel, Helen Hill, Berthe Hunt, and Marie Lange, with gas masks and helmets in hand, moved toward the trenches, where they faced considerable danger. Even so, those left behind bemoaned the fact that they weren't chosen.

As soon as the attack began, the telephone lines were under constant threat, going in and out when thunderstorms and bombs took their toll, requiring repair on the front and patience in the office. For what seemed like an eternity, officers and operators alike were strained to the utmost as they struggled to answer every call. Then, as operator Esther Fresnel said, "All at once, something seemed to come over everybody. [The voices from the battlefield] were not so harsh—[the men] almost said funny things to us over the lines. . . . [A]nd we knew—even before we were told—that the whole thing had been successful."[5]

Shortly after the assault at St. Mihiel, Pershing asked for six more operators to join the original handpicked group, for now an attack on Argonne was in the works. This assault was also successful. Then, as troops made preparations for yet another drive, the war ended.

Pershing praised the operators for the role they had played in his soldiers' victories, calling the women "switchboard soldiers." These soldiers, the first of their kind, regarded their role in the war as the experience of all experiences, one that few of these women—like those in the Navy, Marines, and Coast Guard—would ever forget.

CHAPTER FIVE

CARING *for the* WOUNDED

Our Government provided for the enlistment of nurses, but not for women physicians. This was a mistake. It is utterly impossible to leave a large number of well-trained women out of a service in which they belong, for the reason that they won't stay out.
Dr. Esther Pohl Lovejoy

In all of America's wars, women have helped care for the wounded. The first women to do so volunteered their services during the Revolutionary War. They bandaged soldiers' wounds in makeshift hospitals, administered medications, and carried soup and blankets to sick captives held on ships that had been converted into floating prisons. Although this involved women outside their homes, their work was acceptable because it was seen as an extension of one of their most important housewifely tasks—caring for the health of their families and neighbors.

During the Civil War, when a single battle might claim a thousand casualties in one day, nurses were in great demand. No longer able to rely strictly on a few local volunteers, military leaders in both the North and South decided to take a bold step and hire female nurses, a number of whom had received formal medical training. Even though including women in the medical corps was controversial when the war began—critics were afraid that women were too weak to deal with the trauma of war—the nurses proved that they could handle almost anything. More than three thousand tended hideous wounds, cleaned up filthy hospitals—sometimes single-handedly—and assisted surgeons while they amputated legs and arms.

Since female nurses had proved so valuable during the Civil War, no one questioned the Army's decision to include them in its medical corps when America declared war on Spain in 1898 even if it meant sending women overseas. Approximately 1,500 served in the Spanish-American War in Cuba, Puerto Rico, the Philippine Islands, and on a hospital ship, the *Relief*.

Because the Army had struggled mightily to find enough nurses during the Civil and Spanish-American wars, the War Department finally decided that it would be best to have nurses on duty at all times. That way someone would be on hand to care for enlisted men during peacetime, and if war broke out, the Army and Navy would have at least some nurses they could immediately call upon. So Congress created the Army Nurse Corps in 1901 and the Navy Nurse Corps in 1908.

At the beginning of the Great War, the U.S. armed services were in a difficult position. Because the United States was a neutral nation, neither the Army nor the Navy could officially make plans for all-out war, yet both had to be prepared for the possibility of large-scale combat. There was little the services could do about enlisting men in large numbers or stockpiling weapons, since the War Department lacked the necessary funds to take action. However, the services could take steps to secure medical support. Shortly after Austria declared war on Serbia, the War Department sought the aid of a private organization, the Red Cross.

After numerous discussions, the Red Cross, which was already helping the wounded in Europe, agreed to establish fifty portable base hospitals for the Army. If the United States entered the war, these hospitals would be ready to provide basic care for wounded and sick soldiers well behind the fighting lines, unlike field units that would operate near the front and provide immediate medical assistance for the men most in need. Each base hospital was to have tents, wood floors, cots, bedding, medical equipment, and a professional staff of civilian doctors and nurses, all of whom had been screened and could enlist at a moment's notice. To raise the necessary money, the Red Cross decided to solicit funds from medical groups, professional organizations, and colleges. To

Letters from Julia Catherine Stimson

Julia Catherine Stimson served as the chief nurse of Base Hospital #21 in France for almost a year. During this time, she often wrote to her parents. Below are excerpts from some of her first letters, which reflect a deep desire to serve in the "war to end all wars" and a strong measure of courage.

May 4, 1917—I just wish I had the words to express what I think about this opportunity. . . . [T]o be in the front ranks in this most dramatic event that ever was staged . . . is all too much good fortune for any one person like me. . . . It seems as if my life has just overflowed with good things and that I can never live long enough to put back into the world all that has been given to me.

May 26, 1917—First night in danger zone safely passed and everything O.K.

July 16, 1917—All day yesterday and in the night we heard the booming of guns, and the night nurses say the windows in our surgical hut rattled. It was the loudest I have heard since we have been here.

July 25, 1917—[W]e have begun our hard work, and . . . we are glad for it. . . . Many of the nurses have worked 14 straight hours to-day, and many of the doctors had only two or three hours' sleep last night, and were working all day. . . . Three additional night nurses are on to-night, taken from the day force that has to stretch itself a little thinner.

August 8, 1917—Our hospital is very full and we have many very bad cases. My nurses are beginning to show the effect of the emotional strain.[1]

In mid-1918, Stimson took charge of all Army nurses in France. After the war ended, Julia Catherine Stimson continued to serve in the Army Nurse Corps. She became superintendent of the corps in 1919.

encourage groups to give generously, the Red Cross promised that each organization sponsoring an entire project would have a hospital named in its honor. Twenty-five base hospitals were ready for action when Congress declared war.

While the base hospitals were being organized, some American women who wanted to help win the war joined the Allies. Most went on their own; others were funded by relief organizations. These women served as nurses, doctors, and ambulance drivers in France, England, Russia, and Serbia. How many undertook such a daring adventure is not certain, for they were not included in official records.

One woman, Mary Borden, a wealthy socialite from Chicago, actually started her own hospital in 1914 in a cluster of buildings in France. She described her site as the second battlefield:

> I thought, 'This is the second battlefield. The battle is now going on over the helpless bodies of these men. It is we who are doing the fighting now, with their real enemies.' And I thought of the chief surgeon, the wizard working like lightning through the night, and all the others wielding their flashing knives against the invisible enemy. The wounded had begun to arrive at noon. It was now past midnight, and the door kept opening and shutting to let in the stretcher-bearers, and the ambulances kept lurching in at the gates. Lanterns were moving through the windy dark from shed to shed. The nurses were out there in the scattered huts, putting the men to bed . . . asleep from the operating rooms. . . .
>
> 'We will send you the dying, the desperate, the moribund,' the Inspector-General had said. 'You must expect a thirty percent mortality.' So we got ready for it; we had organized to [fight] that figure.[2]

Mary Borden eventually was joined by thousands of nurses. By 1918 the Army had enrolled 21,000 volunteers and the Navy had 1,200, the majority of whom served overseas. All of these women worked long hours under difficult conditions, but those who served close to the front saw the worst cases. Chief Nurse Julia Stimson worried about the women she assigned to field hospitals. She said:

> What with the steam [used to disinfect operating tools], the ether [an anesthetic], and the filthy clothes of the men . . . the odor in the operating room was so terrible that it was all that any of [the nurses] could do to keep from being sick. One of my nurses was sick at her stomach all night long the first night she worked there . . . but kept right on with her work . . . no mere handing of instruments and sponges, but sewing and tying up and putting in drains while the doctor takes the next piece of shell out of another place. Then after fourteen hours of this, with freezing feet, to a meal of

Field nurses from all countries, including these from Great Britain, sometimes demonstrated their dedication and heroics by administering first aid right in the trenches where the men were injured.

tea and bread and jam, and off to rest if you can in a wet bell tent in a damp bed without sheets. . . . One need never tell me that women can't do as much, stand as much, and be as brave as men.[3]

As the number of serious casualties mounted, field nurses were overwhelmed. Sometimes base hospitals sent staff members to the front during a major battle to help. But this often meant that their own hospitals were then seriously understaffed. For example, at one point, one hospital had only eight nurses to assist two surgeons and care for 1,200 patients. By August 1918, the situation had become so critical that the armed services issued a public plea for more nurses. The services, officials said, needed at least 8,000 volunteers in the next four months.

But even though the situation was critical, the Army and Navy refused to accept black nurses. Both corps insisted that providing separate housing for these women was too much of a problem. So more than 1,800 desperately needed professionals who were willing to serve remained at home.

However, a major outbreak of deadly flu in the fall of 1918, which eventually killed 21 million people worldwide, gave these nurses an opportunity to serve the war effort even though it wasn't exactly as they had planned. The Red Cross hired some of them to help care for flu victims on the home front whose services were vital to the war effort.

Aileen Bertha Cole was one of the chosen few. "The Red Cross," she said, "finally asked us to help during the flu epidemic in 1918. People were dying everywhere. Some of us were asked to go to West Virginia to work among the coal miners, where the epidemic was very serious. We were told, 'We've got to save the miners' lives to keep the transports [ships] moving. If we keep the transports moving, we can keep our boys crossing over. The outcome of the war depends on them, and on you Red Cross nurses.'"[4]

Black nurses weren't the only women in the medical profession who were denied the opportunity to serve overseas. Although there were 6,000 female physicians in the United States in 1917, 40 percent of whom said they would gladly go to the front, they, too, were ignored.

Believing that they could change the official position of the armed services by demonstrating their commitment and professionalism, some female doctors decided to follow the example of the Red Cross and establish a portable hospital, which they would then present, complete with a staff of female physicians, to the government. Two groups agreed to sponsor the project: the New York Infirmary for Women and Children; and Carrie Chapman Catt's organization, the National American Woman Suffrage Association.

But War Department officials, to the women's utter astonishment and dismay, refused the gift. They informed the hospital's organizers that female doctors would be accepted only if they agreed to be contract workers—that is,

After the refusal by the War Department of the United States to accept their services, this first contingent of the Women's Overseas Hospital prepares to serve the French Army, which gladly accepted its offer.

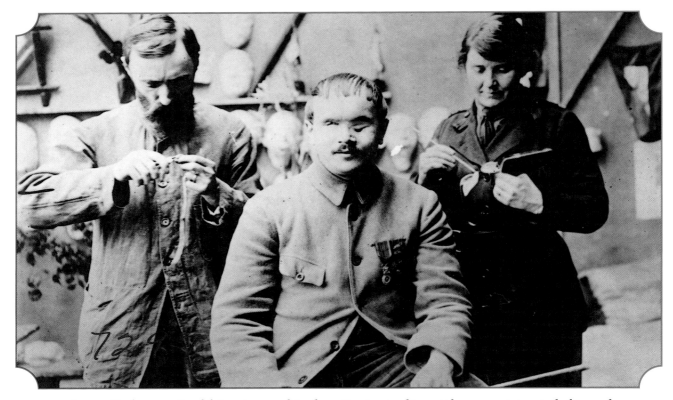

Anna Coleman Ladd is pictured in her Paris studio with an assistant (left) and one of the disfigured soldiers she worked with.

doctors without rank. This meant that, unlike the male physicians, who were part of the Army and therefore given rank, the women could not give orders. In fact, the women couldn't even tell an orderly to perform a task, an impossible and humiliating situation. Miffed and now resigned to not being able to serve in the armed services' medical corps, the organizers of the project offered the Women's Overseas Hospital to the French Army, which gladly accepted the tent, equipment, and staff.

Because more female physicians wanted to go to Europe, the Medical Women's National Association decided to organize, fund, and staff two base hospitals to give these women an opportunity to serve. The first American

Women's Hospital (AWH #1) opened in July 1918 in France. In addition to nurses and doctors, the staff included three dentists. Because this was a private project, the hospital could accept civilians as well as soldiers. For many French citizens, AWH #1 provided the first opportunity to receive medical care since the war broke out, so they flocked to the tent.

Of all the staff members, the dentists were the most popular. "Our work," one of the supervisors said, "will be a joy forever in France—at least as long as our fillings last. . . . A woman dentist had never been seen in that section of France. They were rare creatures, far more interesting than men dentists, their work was just as good."[5]

AWH #2 opened in October under the direction of Dr. Ethel Fraser. Like AWH #1, this hospital served many civilians; unlike AWH #1, female physicians actively sought out patients. They traveled to nearby villages looking for people who were suffering from flu, tuberculosis, and typhoid fever. These doctors did not have to look far. Many civilians, lacking adequate food, shelter, and clean drinking water due to the ravages of war, were easy prey for disease. The demand for medical care was so great that by late 1918, hospital organizers had seventy-eight female physicians on staff to serve in AWH #1 and AWH #2.

Unlike previous wars, after which disabled soldiers were expected to remain in their homes for the rest of their lives, cared for by mothers, sisters, or wives, World War I casualties were given special help so that they might lead somewhat normal lives when the fighting stopped. This help came from approximately eight hundred women who worked in Reconstruction Aide Units, which included physical and occupational therapists. Because these therapists were the first of their kind, doctors and nurses didn't always know how to make the best use of the women's skills. As a result, some of the therapists were little more than nurses' assistants until the therapists' directors objected rather strenuously.

In general, physical therapists helped the wounded rebuild their bodies, or in the case of the loss of a limb, learn how to compensate for the missing arm or leg. Most therapists used heat and massage to relieve pain and encouraged movement and even vigorous exercise. Some resorted to electrical shock when nerves surrounding a wound had been severely damaged. At that time, shock was believed to speed up the healing process.

Occupational therapists taught the men vocational skills. Although some therapists limited their training to teaching the blind to read Braille or the severely wounded how to type, knit, or weave, Mrs. Clyde McDowell Myres undertook a more unorthodox project. Myres turned a vacant building into a workshop. She taught the men how to make chairs and small tables from old wood taken from bombed-out buildings. Because many a telephone operator, clerk, and even some officers were using crates for chairs, the workshop's wood products were in great demand, a fact that heartened the craftsmen.

Although therapists could help rebuild bodies and teach new skills, none could remove the awful facial wounds that so many soldiers had suffered. These wounds were the result of trench warfare. Men's heads were exposed first when they climbed over the top to attack the enemy; therefore, they were the first targets. To make it possible for the disfigured men to appear in public without feeling awkward, another group of specialists was called upon: sculptors who could make portrait masks. Working from photos, mask makers created duplicates of the men's faces before they were injured. One of the best-known American sculptors of the day, Anna Coleman Ladd, set up a studio in Paris under the auspices of the Red Cross. Her masks were widely acclaimed and eagerly sought by injured soldiers.

All of the women who helped the wounded—the nurses, doctors, therapists, and sculptors—gave generously of their time and talent. Many risked their lives to serve, and at least a hundred died, mostly from disease, during the war. Yet few could imagine themselves anywhere else. Nellie Dingley, an Army nurse, spoke for many: "There is a touch of the divine in the manner in which these American boys face everything—wounds, sickness and death—they die smiling. It seems so small a thing for a woman to do—all she can do—and she should do that nobly—stand by them in their last great hour."[6]

CHAPTER SIX

With PEN
IN HAND

I could claim . . . that I wanted to see this war so that I could write against war. . . . But it would not be true. Not then. I had at that time no hatred of war, only a great interest and a great curiosity. All my suppressed sense of adventure, my desire to discover what physical courage I had, my instincts as a writer, had been aroused by what was going on in Europe.
Mary Roberts Rinehart, journalist

Before World War I, few women were war correspondents. During the Revolutionary War, women limited their efforts to showing support for one side or another. Mercy Otis Warren, for example, wrote plays that made fun of the British, while Margaret Draper published a newspaper in Boston praising them.

During the Civil War, many women took pen in hand. Keeping journals then was common, and some of these, which detailed the women's lives during the war, were published after the conflict ended. Mary Chesnut's journal is perhaps the best known of these works, and it is still read today. Also, women who led adventurous lives during the war, spies or soldiers in disguise, published their memoirs when it was safe to do so both to share their exploits with the public and to earn an income. A few women, such as Julia Ward Howe, who composed the words to "The Battle Hymn of the Republic," wrote lyrics to show their support. Meanwhile, Jane Swisshelm, a journalist for the *New York Tribune*, worked as a war correspondent. But she served in Washington, D.C., where she gathered information from wounded soldiers and government officials. She did not go to the front, as war correspondents do today.

When the Great War started, more than a few American women were determined to write about it. Some were living in Europe in 1914, and they took advantage of their position. For instance, Mildred Aldrich, a retired journalist, resided in a small village in France on the Marne River only a few miles from the front. At times she could hear the roar of cannons, and she witnessed trucks and troops passing by. Eventually Aldrich took enough notes about her life in the small village during the conflict to write several books, including *On the Edge of the War Zone*.

Frances Huard was also living in France in 1914. After her husband joined the war effort, Huard turned their château into a hospital and a retreat for Belgian refugees. But her location was far from safe. The Germans were pushing hard to conquer all of France, and Huard's home was on the route the enemy had chosen. When the Germans were only a few miles away, she ordered everyone to abandon her home, then hopped on her bicycle to lead them to safety. As soon as the French pushed the Germans back, she returned to her château. Shortly after, she started a book, *My Home in the Field of Mercy*, which, when published in America in 1916, increased the public's sympathy for the Allies.

Not all American writers in Europe lived in one of the countries that had joined the Allies. Sigrid Schultz lived in Germany. A pipe smoker and a popular hostess, she ran the *Chicago Tribune's* office in Berlin. Schultz, who seldom minced words, incurred the kaiser's wrath when she criticized him. Even so, she was allowed to remain in Berlin, where in the 1930s, this bold woman would anger another German leader, Adolf Hitler, when she warned the former Allies about Hitler's plans to conquer the world.

While a few women were starting to write about some aspect of the war in Europe, others, such as Nellie Bly, were making plans to go there. Bly had already made headlines when she exposed shocking conditions in mental hospitals after arranging to be committed to an institution so she could see firsthand what patients endured. Later she caught the public's attention when she traveled around the world to try to best Jules Verne's fictional Phileas Fogg, who had made the same journey in Verne's book *Around the World in 80 Days*. Bly, using a variety of forms of transportation, broke Fogg's record by eight days. In 1914 she was ready for a new challenge: She wanted to describe the war from a woman's viewpoint. After presenting her latest—and perhaps her most dangerous—project to her editor at the *New York Evening Journal*, he reluctantly agreed to send her.

In August 1914, Nellie Bly, who supported the Central Powers, went to Austria, where she had well-connected friends, including the U.S. ambassador to Austria, Frederic C. Penfield. Bly hoped that her friends would make it possible for her to travel throughout the empire as well as go to the war zone. She was not disappointed, although preparations took much longer than she had anticipated. It took her nearly three months to get her plans and passes in order. Finally, on October 26, she cabled her editor:

> I will send three articles. Now on way to Przemysl. I go to the firing line. Will write all I can and will cable important things when possible. . . . Get up a movement among your readers to send packages of cotton [for bandages] . . . to the Red Cross, War Department [Vienna]. All out here. Poor wounded soldiers suffering. . . . Everything going well with Austria—winning. Everybody—soldiers, officers and officials—splendid.[1]

Bly planned to visit the front between Austria and Russia and the war zone between Austria and Serbia. She was one of six journalists who had been granted permission to make this trip, all of whom had agreed to submit their reports to censors before being provided with passes and guides. After many days of traveling, the journalists abandoned their wagons near a long, muddy road that would lead them to the first front. As they plodded through ankle-high muck, they passed long lines of wounded soldiers who were walking or being carried to the nearest dressing station for medical care. Bly noted that sometimes the soldiers saluted the officer leading the journalists' party, but "more often," she said, "they staggered unconsciously and forlornly on, their sunken eyes fixed pathetically on the west. Blind to their surroundings, their ears deaf to the near and ceaseless thundering of cannons, their nerves dead."[2]

Nellie Bly speaks to an Austrian officer during her time in that country, in which she arranged to travel to the front to do some reporting on the war. Her bias in favor of the Axis powers, however, angered some of her American readers.

As the journalists neared the front, they were fired upon. Bly recorded the terrifying event:

> [Our guide] yelled for us to fly to the trenches. . . .
>
> Another frightful explosion in the east; another cloud of black smoke and one after the other six shells fell and buried themselves in the same soft earth.
>
> Then I got into the trench. . . . I was not afraid. I would not run. Yet my mind was busy. I thought another shot would follow.[3]

She was wrong. Fortunately, no more shells were aimed at the journalists.

After taking many notes and interviewing Austrian troops and prisoners of war, the writers left this front and began a long trek, part by train, part by wagon, toward Serbia. They endured cold weather, poor food, and filthy living conditions. Again, all along the way, horrified at both the suffering of the soldiers and the civilians, Bly took notes to describe what war was really like. When the journalists neared the second front, they were turned away for reasons that are not clear.

By now, the journey, originally estimated to last only two weeks, had turned into a monthlong ordeal. The journalists were exhausted, even the nearly indefatigable Bly, in part because she wore a long and heavy fur coat (she claimed it weighed 50 pounds, or 23 kilograms). As a result, the reporters agreed not to make a second attempt to see this war zone.

Since all material had to be read and approved by a censor, which takes time, Bly's first article did not appear in the *New York Evening Journal* until December 3, 1914. Her column was titled "Nellie Bly on the Firing Line." Although this article was well-received, her bias in favor of Austria angered some readers.

Mary Roberts Rinehart also went to Europe. Writing for the *Saturday Evening Post*, Rinehart covered the war from the Allies' viewpoint. She began by persuading the Belgians to give her a pass. She told Belgian officials that "of invaded Belgium we knew a great deal; of the small Belgian army, of the Belgian refugees pushed ahead of the army and still trying to subsist behind the Allied lines, we knew nothing."[4] Someone, she argued, should write their story, and that someone was Mary Roberts Rinehart. Belgian officials agreed.

Rinehart also accompanied other journalists, all men, when the Belgians agreed to take reporters to what was called No-Man's-Land, a strip of land that separated the trenches of the Allies from those of the Germans. It was an uncomfortable and dangerous trip; the journalists had to walk the last mile through wind and rain, all the while trying to avoid being seen by the Germans. The journey was also newsworthy. This was the first official trip into No-Man's-Land allowed to any correspondents by the Allies.

After filing her story, Rinehart went to England, then back to France, where she ventured to the front again. This time, she wrote about the Battle of the Marne. Unlike several female journalists who would cover future conflicts, Rinehart came to hate war, and by late 1918, she was writing human-interest stories—how soldiers were trained for combat, for instance—far from the front.

Shortly after the Russians had formed a new government in the spring of 1917, several leaders struggled for control of the country. One of these leaders was Vladimir Lenin, who had been living in exile. When the czar was removed from power, Lenin raced back to Russia with the help of Germany's leaders. Lenin, who promised to provide "Peace and Bread" for the Russians, vowed to withdraw Russia from the war if he gained control. He also promised to install an entirely new economic and political system in Russia called communism. He believed that the country's land and wealth should be seized by the government, then given to those who needed it. This idea especially appealed to the poor and landless peasants, of which there were many. In addition, Lenin believed that workers were best able to determine hours and output, so committees of laborers should replace managers. Likewise, Lenin and his followers, called Bolsheviks, thought that once everything was stabilized, committees of ordinary citizens should replace government officials.

Not content to change only Russia, Lenin cast his eyes upon the whole world. He argued that soldiers should stop fighting each other and unite instead. The enemies of the masses, he insisted, were not the common people in other lands. The real adversaries were leaders, who, Lenin said, should be brought to their knees. This idea startled and upset many citizens in other countries, especially those who were rich and powerful.

Needless to say, the struggle in Russia was fascinating, and even though the country was close to civil war, many journalists wanted to go there to record the dramatic events. Among these journalists were Louise Bryant and Rheta Childe

Dorr, both of whom were interested in Lenin and his ideas as well as the role women were playing in the war against the Central Powers.

About 3,500 Russian women had armed themselves, and after a brief training stint, they considered themselves warriors. Bryant interviewed some as they headed to the front to fight the Germans. "I left everything," one woman told Bryant, "because I thought the poor soldiers of Russia were tired after fighting so many years, and I thought we ought to help them."[5]

Rheta Childe Dorr actually accompanied one of the women's battalions to the front. This group, led by Maria Botchkareva, planned to fight until all were dead. As they neared the war zone, they encountered increased hostility from Russian troops who had revolted against the war and were abandoning the battlefield. The women, far from timid, told the men to go back to the front. When they refused to do so, the female warriors shouted, "Go home, you cowards, and let women fight for Russia."[6]

While Bryant and Dorr were interviewing women warriors, Peggy Hull, who would also go to Russia one year later, was struggling to get accreditation from the War Department. If successful, Hull would be able to accompany U.S. troops to the front, a first for a woman. When she approached her editor at the El Paso (Texas) *Morning Times*, he wondered aloud why she couldn't cover the war like other female journalists. He pointed to articles in women's magazines, especially *McCall's* and *Good Housekeeping*. Why couldn't she just go to England as these journalists had and write about women in the British military if she had to write about war? Numerous debates followed, but Hull, determined to go to the front, finally won.

Besides support from her editor, Hull had to have permission from the War Department in order to accompany the troops. Army officials didn't want women in the press corps, at least not at the front. On the other hand, they couldn't ignore Hull; she knew General Pershing and had appealed to him for help in her struggle to go to Europe. To avoid a confrontation, the War Department sidestepped the problem by issuing Hull a passport, which allowed her to go to France, but failed to give her a pass that would have made it possible for her to go to the front.

Hull still thought that she would be in the heart of life-and-death action. When her ship left the dock on June 14, 1917, she wrote: "A certain fatalism caught at my heart and made me stand—gazing at the widening space between

Peggy Hull (1890–1967)

Peggy Hull, born Henrietta Goodnough in Kansas, was an ambitious woman. After reading articles written by Nellie Bly, young Henrietta couldn't imagine anything better than being a reporter. Because Henrietta, who used her nickname, Peggy, in her bylines, had a fascination with war, she was determined to become a war correspondent. Until a conflict came along, though, she worked for various papers, including one in Colorado, where she met and married the first of her three husbands, George Hull. They had a stormy relationship at best, separating shortly after.

Peggy's first opportunity to write about armed conflict came in the spring of 1916. President Wilson had sent troops to Mexico in 1914 when U.S. property there had been threatened. Although American troops were withdrawn in 1915, this intervention did not sit well with many Mexicans. Shortly after, various groups, some of which were little more than bandits, took revenge on Americans, first attacking those living in Mexico, then those living near the border in the United States. The most serious attack took place on March 15, 1916, when a group led by Pancho Villa crossed the border and killed seventeen Americans in Columbus, New Mexico.

Fearing more violence, National Guard units immediately made preparations for war with Mexico, which included training women to handle weapons. Peggy, who at the time worked for the Cleveland (Ohio) *Plain Dealer*, joined her local guard unit. When soldiers were sent to the border under General John J. Pershing, whose orders were to break up bands such as Villa's, Peggy told her editor that she was going along. If he wouldn't sponsor her, she would sponsor herself, she said, selling articles to any paper that would accept.

Peggy accompanied the troops with the halfhearted support of her editor, actually marching through New Mexico for fifteen days to find the enemy. Although she never complained about the strenuous hike to anyone within earshot, her journal indicates that following the troops was arduous. Only her desire to write about war kept her going.

The events along the border reaffirmed Hull's desire to be a war correspondent. Besides writing about the Great War, albeit from Siberia, Hull covered the war between China and Japan in the 1930s. But when the United States entered World War II in 1941, Hull, then fifty-one years old, was too old for the rigors of reporting from the front.

the wharf and the ship like a man, who facing a firing squad, looks beyond their rifles to the green hills. My chance to live. My chance to die."[7]

Shortly after Hull arrived in Paris, she was confined to the area. To make the most of a difficult situation, she filed stories about her struggle to get to Paris and pieces about life in a nearby Army camp. When American troops charged into battle, she was left behind. Deeply disappointed, she returned to El Paso.

Lenin finally seized power in November 1917, and one of his first acts as the new leader of Russia, as promised, was to remove his country from the war. This resulted in an enormous loss of territory, which was turned over to Germany, and alarmed the rest of the Allies. Now Russia's withdrawal meant that Germany, which was already proving to be more powerful than anticipated, was free to put all of its soldiers on the Western Front.

Lenin's control of Russia was far from complete, and he had powerful enemies who were determined to overthrow him, some of whom wanted to reenter the war, defeat Germany, and recover lost territory. The Allies, who had no love for Lenin, wanted to do all they could to help his opponents, including limiting the Bolsheviks' access to arms. The United States had provided vast quantities of supplies to Russia, so in September 1918, 10,000 American troops, along with some British and French soldiers, left for Siberia, a northern province in Russia, to reclaim some of the weapons, which were stored near two ports, Archangel (northern Siberia) and Vladivostok (eastern Siberia). Also, nearly 4,000 Czechs had been trapped in Russia on the Eastern Front. They wanted to continue to fight for the Allies, but in order to do so, they needed transportation out of the country.

After complaining and pleading for accreditation and searching for a new sponsor—her old paper could no longer foot the bill—Peggy Hull was finally granted permission to accompany the American troops bound for Siberia. The department agreed to give her a pass because officials thought there would be little danger on this front and also because few war correspondents wanted to cover a new and surprising aspect of the war. The "real" battles, male war correspondents said with a sneer, were in France.

In October 1918, Hull, arrived in Vladivostok. The port was in total chaos. It was, Hull said, "on the threshold of its blackest period. Twice a victim, first to monarchy and then to anarchy—its people this winter will die by thousands. They are freezing to death now and the coldest weather is still to come."[8]

The battles that Hull had hoped to witness never occurred. The Allied troops simply tried to keep law and order in the ports and locate supplies. They withdrew the following spring. Instead of filing dispatches about battles, Hull wrote dozens of stories about events in the port city. Combat for her during the Great War was limited to fighting the War Department for accreditation and paving the way for female journalists in World War II.

Female Spies

Two of the most famous espionage agents of the war were females, Mata Hari and Edith Cavell.

Marta Hari, the professional name of Margaretha Geertruida Zelle, was born in Holland in 1876. After divorcing her husband of two years, a Dutch Army officer, whom she had married when she was eighteen years old, she moved to Paris. To support herself, she became an exotic dancer—who wasn't afraid to bare all—at private parties. Mata Hari was a beautiful woman, and as word spread about her considerable charms, men begged to be invited to events where she was to appear just to get a glimpse of her.

Because she attracted so many men, including high-ranking military officers, German leaders thought that she had excellent potential as an agent. In 1907 they asked her to spy on their old enemies: French soldiers. Mata Hari agreed to do so. When the Great War erupted, Mata Hari continued to supply the Germans with valuable information. But in early 1917, she came under suspicion. She was arrested shortly after, tried, found guilty of espionage, and executed by French soldiers in October 1917.

Edith Cavell, in contrast to Mata Hari, was a prim, matronly nurse. When Belgium was invaded by the Germans, the forty-nine-year-old Cavell rushed to its major city, Brussels, to train women to care for the wounded at a local hospital.

Hundreds of Allied soldiers had been trapped in Belgium when the Germans took over. Because the Germans wanted to prevent these men from rejoining their units, officials announced that anyone caught helping Allied soldiers get out of Belgium would be shot. Even so, Cavell aided at least two hundred men, often hiding them on the hospital's grounds. Some of these men carried vital information for the Allies that they or Cavell had gathered. Like Mata Hari, Cavell eventually came under suspicion. She was executed by German soldiers in October 1915.

Margaretha Geertruida Zelle, also known as Mata Hari

CHAPTER SEVEN

UNSUNG HEROES

American boys are going to France. We must go with them.
Evangeline Booth, U.S. Salvation Army

Shortly after America entered World War I, the War Department was over-whelmed by the incredible task of mobilizing millions of men, all of whom had to be trained, armed, supplied, and shipped to Europe as quickly as possible. And if that task wasn't daunting enough, because this was the first war in which American soldiers would fight on such a large scale in foreign countries, department officials faced at least four unprecedented problems.

First, the armed forces needed more clothing and medical supplies than American industries could supply. The troops still needed hospital gowns, sur-gical masks, and bandages, and when the weather turned cold, they would need mufflers, mittens, and wool socks. Who would provide these?

Second, to maintain mental and emotional well-being, soldiers had to have breaks from training and combat, which meant a place to go and something to do. Who would provide these sites and services, especially overseas?

Third, in order to win the war, morale had to be high, both on the battlefield and on the home front. To accomplish this, soldiers had to be able to maintain contact with loved ones thousands of miles away. In addition, fighting troops needed visible reminders that their country was behind them. How could these things be done?

A grand spa in Nice, France, is transformed into a canteen by the YMCA, where American soldiers on leave could relax, socialize, and get a hot meal. These were important considerations for keeping morale high.

And fourth, the demand for food by the Allies, the American soldiers, and the home front was more than American farmers could fill. Where would more food come from?

Many volunteer organizations were eager to answer the department's questions, and those who offered the best solutions were given the most responsibilities. These included the Red Cross, the Young Men's Christian Association (YMCA), and the Salvation Army.

The efforts of these groups were coordinated and controlled by the War Department, which set high standards for men and women who would have direct contact with the troops. In addition to being at least twenty-five years of age, workers had to produce references that vouched for their personal conduct. Also, because government funds were limited at the moment, if volunteers planned to serve overseas, they had to have enough money to pay for their passage to Europe and, if their organization couldn't afford to provide housing and meals, enough money to pay for room and board as well.

Once activities were coordinated, the three organizations began to cast about for workers and money. Since most men were employed or were potential recruits for the armed services and most young women were working or already serving as yeomanettes or members of one of the nursing corps, all eyes turned toward the last large group of untapped workers: married women.

The Red Cross had been involved in the war effort from the beginning of the conflict, establishing base hospitals and recruiting nurses. Now it actively sought women with cooking skills who could prepare sandwiches and coffee and distribute them at all major railroad stations to recruits bound for training or the front. In addition, the Red Cross sought women who could staff kitchens on wheels in Europe to provide the troops with lemonade, cocoa, and baked goods, something a soldier's rations did not include. Some of these kitchens were little more than wagons with small portable stoves, which followed the men as they advanced. During the battle at St. Mihiel, when telephone operators were first moved to the front, Red Cross volunteers made and served 160,000 gallons (605,648 liters) of hot cocoa.

To provide supplies that industries couldn't, the Red Cross corralled women on the home front who could sew or operate cutting machines. In six weeks, seamstresses made 400,000 gowns for patients and thousands of comfort bags, which were stuffed with toothpaste, soap, and razors. These bags were especially important because most patients did not arrive with their personal belongings, and the government did not provide these necessities. Meanwhile, other volunteers used cutting machines to trim large pieces of gauze, cotton, and linen into standardized shapes, which could then be folded or rolled into bandages. During the same six-week period, volunteers turned out 3,600,000 surgical dressings.

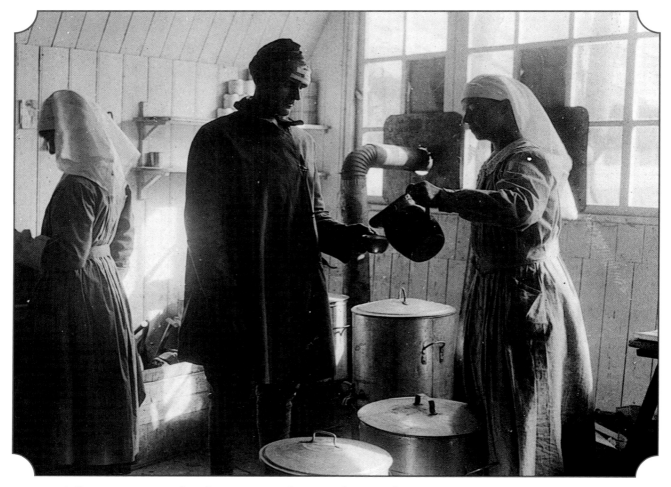

This emergency kitchen at a Red Cross hospital in France served hot cocoa to a thousand wounded soldiers a day.

To help meet the need for extra clothing for the winter months, Red Cross volunteers encouraged all women who knew how to knit to make garments for the soldiers. Thousands of signs were posted that said: "Our boys need sox. Knit your bit." The first volunteers apparently knew how to make footwear, but a little later, when some goods with pointy heels and toes began to show up in donation boxes, leaders decided to offer knitting classes.

The Red Cross concentrated on the health of the troops and sent approximately 4,500 women to Europe to work in rolling kitchens and hospital tents. The YMCA focused primarily on the social needs of the soldiers, setting up canteens in the United States and overseas. The canteens gave soldiers a place to play cards, read, visit with other soldiers in a relaxed setting, and purchase a homestyle meal (meat, mashed potatoes and gravy, vegetable, bread, and dessert) for fifteen cents. In July 1917, when the Y began to accept female volunteers, canteens hosted dances as well.

Y volunteers also established leave centers in Europe, far from the front. These centers provided soldiers, who were given a week's break from fighting, with a variety of activities: hiking, swimming, golfing, playing tennis, and taking in a moving picture or two, the latest in modern entertainment. The first centers were started by Mrs. Vincent Astor and Mrs. Theodore Roosevelt Jr., both of whom were in France when the Great War started. They were eventually joined by 3,500 other women. By the end of the war, there were 23 leave centers in Europe and hundreds of Y canteens.

Unlike the Red Cross and the YMCA, the Salvation Army was met with skepticism when it offered its services to the war effort. For years, many Americans had considered this army little more than a religious group. How, critics wondered, would it be of practical value to the soldiers? Even though the army's commander, Evangeline Booth, met stiff resistance, she eventually convinced the War Department to give her organization a chance to provide social and recreational opportunities for the troops as well as religious services, which, Commander Booth had pointed out when pleading for a chance to serve, weren't necessarily a bad thing.

As soon as Booth received permission to participate in the effort, she and her volunteers started canteens near training centers wherever the Y had not done so. Each site, called a hut, was meant to be a social center for enlisted men. By the end of the war, the Salvation Army had ninety-one huts in the United States.

Next, Booth organized a fact-finding mission. Eleven members—seven men and four women—under Lieutenant Colonel William Barker, toured France to determine how best to serve the soldiers there. Barker concluded that huts that could serve baked goods, provide writing supplies and stamps so soldiers could stay in touch with loved ones, and offer a clothes-mending service were in great

YMCA Volunteers
Addie Hunton and Kathryn M. Johnson

Although many black women tried to serve their country during the Great War, few were allowed to do so. Addie Hunton and Kathryn M. Johnson, social workers, were the exception. Both women were assigned to YMCA canteens in France, where they served black soldiers. Hunton and Johnson wrote about their year in Europe in a book titled *Two Colored Women with the A.E.F.* Here are excerpts from the text:

The Paris Headquarters of the Young Men's Christian Association cabled as follows: 'Send six fine colored women at once!'. . .

Six women! A small number to be sure, but the requirements for eligibility were not so easy to meet and one must not have a close relative in the army. Many questions were asked. 'Was there a real need for women over there?' 'Could they stand the test?' 'Would they not be subjected to real danger?'. . .

A few leaders were far-visioned enough to see the wisdom of colored women going overseas. [They] . . . worked untiringly to help secure the required number. . . .

[Mrs. James Curtis, Addie Hunton, a widow, and Kathryn Johnson were the first to be given permission to go.]

The huts were crowded and the canteen lines unending. . . . Those were busy but happy days! . . .

[A] man stood near the canteen one day, but not in line. He stood so quietly and so long that we finally asked if we could serve him. He simply gave a negative shake of the head. After several minutes we said, 'Surely you desire something,' only to be met by another shake of the head. The third time we inquired he said quietly, 'Lady, I just want to look at you, if you charge anything for it I'll pay you—it takes me back home.'[1]

Kathryn Johnson stands with some of the black soldiers she served at a YMCA canteen in France.

Women Helping Women

Soldiers were not the only Americans who needed support during the war; many women found themselves in unusual circumstances due to the conflict, and they, too, needed help. One of the most active support groups for this population was the Young Women's Christian Association (YWCA). This organization, which sent 350 women overseas, provided recreation sites for nurses in the Army and Navy Nurse Corps, found housing for women in the Signal Corps, a nearly impossible feat since so many buildings were in ruins near the front, and ran a hotel in Paris complete with hot water and bubble bath, where Red Cross, YMCA, and Salvation Army volunteers could rest for a few days.

The YWCA also supported women affected by the war in the United States. It provided counselors for women in industry who found themselves overwhelmed in their new jobs and located housing for women who relocated to take positions in war industries. In addition, the YWCA ran hostess houses near training camps, where mothers, sisters, wives, and girlfriends could stay for a few days while visiting soldiers about to be shipped overseas. And finally, Y volunteers provided housing in Europe and moral support for any American woman who wanted to visit the grave of a son, brother, husband, or boyfriend who had died in the war.

need. Staff members, six per hut, Baker said, should include four female volunteers who could "mother" the boys.

Lacking the necessary funds to start huts overseas, Commander Booth borrowed $125,000, a sum that stunned members. How, they asked Booth, would the organization ever pay off such a huge debt? Booth replied, "It is only a question of our getting to work in France, and the American public will see that we have all the money we want."[2]

Approximately 250 Salvation Army volunteers, supported by the Salvation Army's War Service League in America, 31,000 strong, went to France. Because the Salvation Army followed the troops, usually setting up huts in abandoned buildings, providing food that needed to be cooked in ovens was difficult at best. Wanting to offer treats of some kind, Ensign Margaret Sheldon and Adjutant Helen Purviance decided to make doughnuts, which could be fried in hot fat over portable stoves. The doughnuts were an instant hit, and soon many soldiers were visiting Salvation Army huts. On one particularly busy day, Margaret Sheldon wrote: "Today I made 22 pies, 300 doughnuts, 700 cups of coffee."[3]

Distributing homemade doughnuts

Salvation Army volunteers worked wherever they were needed to bring aid and comfort to the fighting men.

Writing a letter home for a wounded soldier

Making pies

More Women at War

American women were not the only females to try to help their side win the Great War. Several million women, especially those living in the countries that were among the first to declare war, became deeply involved in this conflict.

For example, although women in Germany held few manufacturing jobs in 1914, in 1918 they accounted for 28 percent of the workforce, most of which was producing guns and bullets. In France, women held more than 40 percent of the manufacturing jobs in 1918, and in Great Britain the number of working women soared from approximately 200,000 at the beginning of the war to 950,000 in 1918, when women were making more than 80 percent of all weapons and shells used by British troops.

Many European women also worked hard to try to provide food for their soldiers and loved ones at home. In Great Britain, 250,000 joined the Land Army, which planted, tended, and harvested crops. Meanwhile, Frenchwomen took over farms far from the front when their husbands, brothers, or fathers went off to war.

Although food was limited in Great Britain and France, few people faced starvation. But in Germany and Austria, the situation was much more serious. Both nations had long relied on other countries for a large portion of their foodstuffs. When the war broke out, the Allies blockaded the Central Powers, making importing food almost impossible. To make up for the shortages, women raised vegetables in small plots in their yards, picked through harvested fields in hopes of finding overlooked produce, and used every edible item, including potato peelings, when preparing meals. The mortality rate for German women rose from 11 percent in 1914 to 30 percent in 1918, due in large part to the lack of food.

Many women of various nationalities also served near or at the front. Women from each warring country risked their lives to tend the wounded, while 3,500 Russian women bore arms on the battlefield. Because it was socially acceptable for a Serbian woman to take the place of a loved one when he died in combat, historians believe that at least some of these women also fought.

Many soldiers wrote home about the Salvation Army's work, which had a dramatic effect on the public's opinion of the organization. When it held a fund drive in 1918, hoping to raise a million dollars, Americans donated twice that sum.

One did not have to be a member of the Red Cross, YMCA, or Salvation Army to help the war effort. Thousands of women provided aid through women's organizations such as the Federation of Women's Clubs, the Daughters of the American Revolution, and the Council of Jewish Women. Some of these organizations raised money to purchase medical supplies for American soldiers as well as Allied war victims. Others raised fruits and vegetables when it became clear that farmers could produce only so much food and the home front was running short. These groups turned vacant lots all over the country into gardens, producing $350 million worth of food in one growing season.

Even individual women without the benefit of an organization made significant contributions. They supported friends and neighbors when their sons or daughters were in the war zone, joined in "wheatless" and "meatless" days when, in order to have more food to send to the front, citizens volunteered to do without a designated food one day a week, and spent hundreds of hours rounding up scrap paper and used tin foil to give to the government for reuse. When bond drives were held, a million women, including garment workers who had little money to spare, bought a bond or two, providing the government with funds for the war effort. No books or plaques list the names of these ordinary women, yet like the volunteers for the Red Cross, YMCA, the Salvation Army, and countless other organizations, all of them, in their own ways, were unsung heroes.

CHAPTER EIGHT

AFTERWORD

I cannot understand what it is all about or what has been accomplished by all this waste of youth.

Alice Lord O'Brian, canteen director

On November 11, 1918, Germany, due to recent losses on the battlefield, was forced to sign an armistice. The Great War was finally over.

As soon as the guns were silent, the Allies and the Central Powers began to tally their costs; the results were almost unbelievable. At least 8 million soldiers had died, and millions more had been wounded, many of whom were handicapped for life.

Civilians had fared no better. More than 22 million had died due to bombings, famine, and disease. Because so many men, women, and children in the warring nations in Europe lacked access to clean drinking water, adequate food, and medical care, more lives were at risk.

Few countries could help the struggling victims. Money was scarce even among the victorious Allies (a staggering 400 billion dollars had been spent on the war), and governments were shaky at best in Germany, Austria-Hungary, and Russia, as new leaders, who had replaced royal dynasties, struggled for control. To add to the confusion and pain, the successful Allied nations were drawing new borders, and large groups of people suddenly found themselves citizens of a different country. In short, as both the victors and the vanquished looked about, they saw widespread misery. And if they listened carefully, they heard vows of revenge.

To avoid the formation of powerful alliances and the military buildup of the late 1800s that had contributed so heavily to the causes of the Great War, long before the fighting ended President Woodrow Wilson had proposed a peace plan that included limiting arms and establishing an international organization to settle disputes peacefully. Ideally, this organization would be made up of representatives from all nations.

But some American politicians were skeptical about Wilson's proposal. They didn't like the idea of limiting arms at the very moment that Vladimir Lenin was encouraging worldwide revolution. Wilson's opponents also feared joining an international organization. These critics believed that America's enemies might take control and make decisions that were harmful to the security of the United States. The naysayers eventually gained the upper hand. Although an international organization, the League of Nations (the forerunner of the United Nations), was established, the United States did not become a member.

Watching their leaders fight over entry into the League upset Americans. This was not the scene they had envisioned at the end of "the war to end all wars." In fact, many wondered if anything had been accomplished by all the bloodshed and sacrifice if people still couldn't work together. Disillusioned and bitter, many men and women simply wanted to forget about the war and return to the way things were before 1914.

This attitude had a profound effect on the women who had been involved in the war effort, especially the women in industry, yeomanettes, operators in the Signal Corps, and medical personnel and volunteers who had served overseas. Employers urged women who had taken nontraditional jobs in plants that had manufactured war matériel to go home when the armistice was signed. Although defense industries would retool so that they could manufacture peacetime goods, there would be fewer jobs available, and these, manufacturers believed, should go to the returning male veterans. One employer said: "Our men came first before the war, why not now?"[1]

However, women in industry didn't want to give up their jobs. Many, especially black women, had taken dirty and dangerous positions to prove themselves. They had hoped not only to remain with their employers but also had anticipated better jobs in the future.

Many female employees decided to fight for their positions, only to learn that they were on their own. Since the federal government was no longer placing orders with manufacturers, federal officials could offer only limited help. The WTUL had lost some of its clout when the war ended because women workers were no longer in demand, and most unions dominated by men were not eager to help women. As a result, many who had taken positions outside the garment industry lost their jobs. If women didn't quit, they were fired.

This forced most women who wanted to work or needed to do so to take traditional jobs once again. The number of women in secretarial positions increased in the coming years, as did the number of female telephone operators who could barely keep up with the growing list of subscribers.

From the beginning, yeomanettes and the overseas operators had understood that their positions were for the duration of the war. Even so, they expected, but did not receive, official recognition for what they had done. In addition, because the women in the Signal Corps had risked their lives, they regarded themselves as veterans. However, when they applied for benefits, they were told that as far as the Army was concerned, they had been hired as civilians and therefore weren't eligible. Angry at what they considered more than a mere slight, the operators fought for almost sixty years to gain recognition and compensation. In 1977, Congress finally acknowledged the women's contribution to the war effort. By that time, that youngest switchboard soldier was eighty years old.

Although some nurses, doctors, and volunteers remained in Europe to help civilians there, the vast majority returned to America with the soldiers. Many of these women were exhausted, and those who had served in field hospitals or in huts near the front in the cold and mud had severe health problems.

Because this was the first world war, few people on the home front could really understand what overseas workers had seen and endured. Instead, friends and family members expected these women to be their old selves, which was impossible. No longer running at an exhilarating full pitch, carrying images of death and destruction in their minds, and returning to a home front that wanted to forget the war—and therefore the sacrifice these women had made—had a predictable outcome for the workers: depression. Nurses, doctors, and overseas volunteers suffered, as did soldiers, from what became known, several wars later, as post-traumatic stress disorder.

But all was not lost. Even before the war had ended, suffragists believed that the growing list of women's accomplishments overseas and on the home front made it more likely than ever that legislators could finally be persuaded to give women the right to vote. The National American Woman Suffrage Association, under the direction of Carrie Chapman Catt, intensified its drive for the ballot by lobbying legislators in Washington, D.C., and in state legislatures.

At the same time, the National Woman's Party (NWP) strengthened its crusade for the ballot. This group was considered radical in its day, and unlike Catt's group, it had refused to support America's entry into World War I until women were recognized as full-fledged citizens. Instead, the NWP waged a war of its own on the home front to draw attention to its cause. Members, sometimes as many as a thousand at a time, picketed the White House, demanding to know what the president was going to do about women's suffrage, a cause he had claimed to support when the Great War began and the country needed the help of millions of women. Eventually, scuffles broke out between pickets and spectators who had come to heckle the women; before the dust had settled, more than a hundred NWP members had been arrested. This made national headlines.

To demonstrate their deep commitment to their cause, imprisoned NWP women went on a hunger strike. In order to prevent these women from starving to death and becoming martyrs, officials force-fed the women. Revolting images of funnels jammed into women's mouths or long tubes forced down the women's throats and then flooded with liquid flashed through Americans' minds, creating widespread sympathy and support for both the prisoners and their mission.

On January 10, 1918, Representative Jeannette Rankin introduced an amendment to the U.S. Constitution that would make it possible for all women, not just a few in select states, to cast a ballot. Once again, all eyes in the House of Representatives were upon her, just as they had been nine months before when she had refused to vote for war. But this time, Rankin was in the majority. Her amendment received the necessary two-thirds vote to pass.

However, it took the Senate more than a year even to debate the issue. The amendment wasn't passed in that chamber until June 1919.

There is no doubt that the valiant contributions of women to the war effort furthered their cause to gain suffrage. These women celebrate the ratification of the Nineteenth Amendment in August 1920, not quite two years after the close of the war.

Three-fourths of the state legislatures or state conventions (thirty-five in all) had to ratify the amendment before it could go into effect. To increase the chances of this happening, both the National American Woman Suffrage Association and the National Woman's Party worked harder than ever. Arguing for simple justice, members lobbied local legislators until the officials and suffragists were exhausted. Their hard work paid off. On August 26, 1920, Tennessee, the last state needed, ratified the Nineteenth Amendment. This successfully ended a seventy-two-year fight for the ballot.

The importance of the moment was best expressed by Carrie Chapman Catt: "We are no longer petitioners, we are not wards of the nation, but free and equal citizens."[2] It was nothing less than a spectacular victory for women, one in which every extraordinary woman of World War I could claim a part.

TIMELINE

1914   Archduke Francis Ferdinand and his wife, Sophie, are assassinated on June 28.

Austria declares war on Serbia on July 28.

Germany declares war on Russia on August 1.

Germany invades Belgium on August 4, then France. Great Britain declares war on Germany.

Mary Borden makes plans for a hospital near the Western Front in August.

On September 10, the German advance toward Paris is stopped at the Battle of the Marne by the French and British. Both sides literally dig in for a long fight. American women living in Europe, Mildred Aldrich, Francis Huard, and Sigrid Schultz, begin to write about the war. Others, such as Mary Roberts Rinehart, make plans to go to France.

On September 12, trench warfare begins.

Deadlock on the Western Front begins on November 15. This will last for four years. In December, Nellie Bly's first war dispatches are published.

1915   Great Britain attempts to limit shipments of goods bound for Germany by mining the North Sea on February 2.

On February 4, Germany announces unrestricted submarine warfare. Any ship bound to or from an Allied port is now at risk.

The International Congress of Women meets in the Netherlands on April 28. Representatives from the Woman's Peace Party attend.

On May 7, a German U-boat sinks the *Lusitania*, killing 128 Americans.

1916   On March 16, Pancho Villa leads a raid on Columbus, New Mexico. Shortly after, Brigadier-General John J. Pershing is told to capture Villa. Peggy Hull announces that she will accompany the troops as a correspondent.

The United States demands that Germany end its policy of unrestricted submarine warfare on April 18. Germany agrees to do so.

1917   Germany resumes unrestricted submarine warfare in February. Shortly after, the United States breaks diplomatic relations.

On March 1, details of the Zimmermann telegram are released.

On March 12, Czar Nicholas II is forced to step down. Russian leaders start a new government. First female journalists to cover events in Russia make plans to go there.

Three American ships are sunk by German U-boats on March 16.

Secretary of the Navy Josephus Daniels authorizes recruiters to accept women for the Naval Reserve on March 19. The first of 11,000 yeomanettes begin to enlist shortly after.

On April 6, the United States declares war on Germany. Jeannette Rankin votes against the declaration of war. The Red Cross, YMCA, and Salvation Army offer their services. The search for volunteers begins.

The Women's Trade Union League meets on June 9. The WTUL sets standards for female workers.

General John J. Pershing and his staff arrive in France on June 13.

First American Expeditionary Forces arrive in Europe on June 26 with Army and Navy nurses and Red Cross portable hospitals.

Russian troops begin to abandon the front in July.

In November, Lenin and the Bolsheviks overthrow the new government in Russia. Lenin withdraws Russia from the war shortly after.

1918   On March 1, the first female telephone operators sail for Europe.

On June 18, the first Reconstruction Aides begin their work.

In early July, American Women's Hospital #1 opens in France.

On September 12, American soldiers begin the drive that destroys the German lines at St. Mihiel.

Allied troops are sent to Siberia in September.

Deadly flu epidemic hits the United States in the fall. Black nurses are hired by the Red Cross to care for workers vital to the war effort.

In October, American Women's Hospital #2 opens in France.

Peggy Hull arrives in Siberia in November.

The Great War (World War I) ends on November 11.

1920   On August 26, the Nineteenth Amendment is ratified. Women vote in the fall election.

NOTES

Chapter One

1. Henry Steele Commager, editor, *Documents of American History* (New York: Appleton-Century-Crofts, Inc., 1958), pp. 308–312.

2. Hannah Josephson, *Jeannette Rankin, First Lady in Congress* (Indianapolis: The Bobbs-Merrill Company, Inc., 1974), p. 76.

3. Josephson, p. 76.

Chapter Two

1. Rosalyn Baxandall, Linda Gordon, and Susan Reverby, compilers and editors, *America's Working Women* (New York: Random House, 1976), pp. 153, 154.

2. Hannah Josephson, *Jeannette Rankin, First Lady in Congress* (Indianapolis: The Bobbs-Merrill Company, Inc., 1974), p. 77.

Chapter Three

1. Maurine Weiner Greenwald, *Women, War, and Work: The Impact of World War I on Women Workers in the United States* (Ithaca, NY: Cornell University Press, 1990), p. 76.

2. Greenwald, p. 139.

3. Michael V. Uschan, *A Multicultural Portrait of World War I* (New York: Marshall Cavendish, 1996), p. 36.

4. David M. Kennedy, *Over Here: The First World War and American Society* (New York: Oxford University Press, 1980), p. 285.

Chapter Four

1. Linda Grant De Pauw, *Battle Cries and Lullabies: Women in War from Prehistory to the Present* (Norman: University of Oklahoma Press, 1998), p. 225.
2. Lettie Gavin, *American Women in World War I: They Also Served* (Niwot: University Press of Colorado, 1997), p. 2.
3. Gavin, p. 3.
4. De Pauw, p. 227.
5. Gavin, p. 88.

Chapter Five

1. Julia C. Stimson, *Finding Themselves: The Letters of an American Army Chief Nurse in a British Hospital in France* (New York: The Macmillan Company, 1918), pp. 3, 14, 71, 92.
2. Yvonne M. Kline, editor, *Beyond the Home Front: Women's Autobiographical Writing of the Two World Wars* (New York: New York University Press, 1997), p. 70.
3. Stimson, p. 142.
4. Lettie Gavin, *American Women in World War I: They Also Served* (Niwot: University Press of Colorado, 1997), p. 60.
5. Dorothy Schneider and Carl J. Schneider, *Into the Breach: American Women Overseas in World War I* (New York: Viking Penguin, 1991), p. 91.
6. Gavin, p. 63.

Chapter Six

1. Brooke Kroeger, *Nellie Bly: Daredevil, Reporter, Feminist* (New York: Times Books, 1994), pp. 396, 397.
2. Kroeger, p. 399.
3. Kroeger, p. 401.
4. Dorothy Schneider and Carl J. Schneider, *Into the Breach: American Women Overseas in World War I* (New York: Viking Penguin, 1991), p. 209.
5. Schneider and Schneider, p. 225.
6. Schneider and Schneider, p. 227.

7. Wilda M. Smith and Eleanor A. Bogart, *The Wars of Peggy Hull: The Life and Times of a War Correspondent* (El Paso: Texas Western Press, 1991), p. 75.

8. Smith and Bogart, p. 144.

Chapter Seven

1. Yvonne M. Kline, editor, *Beyond the Home Front: Women's Autobiographical Writing of the Two World Wars* (New York: New York University Press, 1997), pp. 103–107.

2. Herbert A. Wisbey, *Soldiers Without Swords: A History of the Salvation Army* (New York: Macmillan, 1955), p. 161.

3. Lettie Gavin, *American Women in World War I: They Also Served* (Niwot: University Press of Colorado, 1997), p. 215.

Chapter Eight

1. Maurine Weiner Greenwald, *Women, War, and Work: The Impact of World War I on Women Workers in the United States* (Ithaca, NY: Cornell University Press, 1990), p. 131.

2. Sarah Jane Deutsch, *From Ballots to Breadlines: American Women 1920–1940* (New York: Oxford University Press, 1994), pp. 21, 22.

BIBLIOGRAPHY

Baxandall, Rosalyn, and Linda Gordon and Susan Reverby, compilers and editors. *America's Working Women*. New York: Random House, 1976.

Breuer, William B. *War and American Women: Heroism, Deeds, and Controversy*. Westport, CT: Praeger, 1997.

Clarke, Ida Clyde. *American Women and the World War*. New York: D. Appleton and Company, 1918.

Commager, Henry Steele, editor. *Documents of American History*. New York: Appleton-Century-Crofts, Inc., 1958.

Crankshaw, Edward. *The Fall of the House of Habsburg*. New York: The Viking Press, 1963.

De Pauw, Linda Grant. *Battle Cries and Lullabies: Women in War from Prehistory to the Present*. Norman: University of Oklahoma Press, 1998.

Deutsch, Sarah Jane. *From Ballots to Breadlines: American Women 1920–1940*. New York: Oxford University Press, 1994.

Gavin, Lettie. *American Women in World War I: They Also Served*. Niwot: University Press of Colorado, 1997.

Gilbo, Patrick F. *The American Red Cross: The First Century*. New York: Harper & Row, 1981.

Greenwald, Maurine Weiner. *Women, War, and Work: The Impact of World War I on Women Workers in the United States*. Ithaca, NY: Cornell University Press, 1990.

Hancock, Joy Bright. *Lady in the Navy: A Personal Reminiscence.* Annapolis: The Naval Institute Press, 1972.

Holm, Maj. Gen. Jeanne Holm. *Women in the Military: An Unfinished Revolution.* Novato, CA: Presidio Press, 1982.

Josephson, Hannah. *Jeannette Rankin, First Lady in Congress.* Indianapolis: The Bobbs-Merrill Company, Inc., 1974.

Kennedy, David M. *Over Here: The First World War and American Society.* New York: Oxford University Press, 1980.

Kline, Yvonne M., editor. *Beyond the Home Front: Women's Autobiographical Writing of the Two World Wars.* New York: New York University Press, 1997.

Kroeger, Brooke. *Nellie Bly: Daredevil, Reporter, Feminist.* New York: Times Books, 1994.

McKinley, Edward H. *Marching to Glory: The History of the Salvation Army in the United States of America, 1880–1980.* San Francisco: Harper & Row, 1980.

Morin, Isobel V. *Women Chosen for Public Office.* Minneapolis: The Oliver Press, Inc., 1995.

Peck, Mary Gray. *Carrie Chapman Catt.* New York: H.W. Wilson Company, 1944.

Schneider, Dorothy and Carl J. *Into the Breach: American Women Overseas in World War I.* New York: Viking Penguin, 1991.

Smith, Karen Manners. *New Paths to Power: American Women 1890–1920.* New York: Oxford University Press, 1994.

Smith, Page. *America Enters the World: A People's History of the Progressive Era and World War I.* Volume 7. New York: McGraw-Hill, 1985.

Smith, Wilda M., and Eleanor A. Bogart. *The Wars of Peggy Hull: The Life and Times of a War Correspondent.* El Paso: Texas Western Press, 1991.

Stimson, Julia C. *Finding Themselves: The Letters of an American Army Chief Nurse in a British Hospital in France.* New York: The Macmillan Company, 1918.

Uschan, Michael V. *A Multicultural Portrait of World War I.* New York: Marshall Cavendish, 1996.

Wisbey, Herbert A. *Soldiers Without Swords: A History of the Salvation Army.* New York: Macmillan, 1955.

FURTHER READING

For more information about the war itself, check out *America in World War I* by Edward F. Dolan (Brookfield, CT: The Millbrook Press, 1996); *World War I* by Peter Bosco (New York: Facts On File, 1991); and *World War I: The War to End All Wars* by Zachary Kent (Hillside, NJ: Enslow, 1994). These books explain why America entered the war; examine the major battles, how they were fought and who won; and describe the various weapons used in combat, including some, such as tanks, that were employed for the first time.

If greater detail is wanted, study *The Marshall Cavendish Illustrated Encyclopedia of World War I* (New York: Marshall Cavendish, 1984). This twelve-volume set is especially useful for information about the war before the United States entered the conflict, and about Lenin and the Russian Revolution.

Unfortunately, there are few books written for young adults about any of the various roles women played in the war. However, there are some good biographies about women who are mentioned in this text. To learn more about Nellie Bly, read *Making Headlines* by Kathy Lynn Emerson (Minneapolis: Dillon Press, 1989) and *Nellie Bly: Daredevil Reporter* by Charles Fredeen (Minneapolis: Lerner, 2000). For more information about Jane Addams, see *Jane Addams: Nobel Prize*

Winner and Founder of Hull House by Bonnie C. Harvey (Berkeley Heights, NJ: Enslow, 1999) and *Peace and Bread* by Stephanie S. McPherson (Minneapolis: Carolrhoda Books, 1993). And finally, Bryna J. Fireside devotes a chapter to Jeannette Rankin in her book *Is There a Woman in the House—or Senate?* (Morton Grove, IL: A. Whitman & Company, 1994). It gives a good summary of the problems that Rankin faced as America's first woman in Congress.

INDEX

J   Zeinert, Karen.
940.3   Those extraordinary women of World Wa
Zei   I
c.2
         00068371

Appomattox Regional Library Systems
Hopewell, Virginia 23860
08/02